The Roman Games

*A Captivating Guide to the Gladiators,
Chariot Races, and Games in Ancient Rome*

Free Bonus from Captivating History (Available for a Limited time)

Hi History Lovers!

Now you have a chance to join our exclusive history list so you can get your first history ebook for free as well as discounts and a potential to get more history books for free! Simply visit the link below to join.

Captivatinghistory.com/ebook

Also, make sure to follow us on Facebook, Twitter and Youtube by searching for Captivating History.

Contents

INTRODUCTION: CRUELTY OF THE AGES? 1

CHAPTER 1 - WHERE DID THE GAMES BEGIN? 5

CHAPTER 2 - POLITICAL AND RELIGIOUS IMPLICATIONS OF THE GAMES 13

CHAPTER 3 - THE GLADIATORS OF THE ROMAN GAMES 21

CHAPTER 4 - SPARTACUS FIGHTS FOR FREEDOM 30

CHAPTER 5 - CHRISTIANS AND THE ROMAN GAMES 38

CHAPTER 6 - EXTRAVAGANT MILITARY REENACTMENTS 53

CHAPTER 7 - COMMODUS: THE EMPEROR TURNED GLADIATOR 60

CHAPTER 8 - CHARIOT RACES: THE ROMAN INDY 500 66

CHAPTER 9 - THE GLADIATRIX: FEMALE GLADIATORS IN THE ARENA 74

CHAPTER 10 - ROME'S ANIMAL-BASED GAMES 79

CHAPTER 11 - ROMAN THEATER IN THE ROMAN GAMES 86

CONCLUSION: THE ROMAN GAMES COME TO AN END 91

HERE'S ANOTHER BOOK BY CAPTIVATING HISTORY THAT YOU MIGHT LIKE 93

FREE BONUS FROM CAPTIVATING HISTORY (AVAILABLE FOR A LIMITED TIME) 94

APPENDIX A: FURTHER READING AND REFERENCE 95

Introduction: Cruelty of the Ages?

It has long been hard for historians to reconcile the greatness of Rome with the cruelty of the arena. On the one hand, the Romans were clearly intelligent empire builders. They could conquer just as easily as they could establish sensible laws and practice virtuous philosophies. Yet, these highly civilized people had no problem at all with two men killing each other to the excited shouts of their fellow Romans in the arena.

Gladiators have been in vogue since the early days of the Roman Republic, and once you throw in a few lions, tigers, and bears (oh my!) inside a huge colosseum, you truly have a spectacle on your hands. Those condemned to fight in the arena were considered criminals of the state, but one must remember that what Rome considered to be criminal behavior is something we might not today.

Christians, after all, were considered criminals simply for their religious beliefs, partly due to their refusal to offer sacrifices to the prosperity of the emperor. As writer and historian Alison Futrell put it, the Christians were condemned simply for "refusing to participate in public religion." Romans publicly offered sacrifices to both their gods and their emperor; Christians were, therefore, quite conspicuous for their refusal to do so.

In fact, they were considered unpatriotic zealots, and they were made to pay a heavy price for their religious convictions. Emperor Nero of Rome would famously blame the Christians for Rome's "Great Fire" in 64 CE, and for the next few centuries or so, Christians would be widely perceived as treacherous enemies of the state.

But besides the Christians and other religious and political dissidents who were thrown to the lions, others condemned to participate in the games were most likely criminals as we would classify them today. Murderers, robbers, rapists, and the like were routinely trotted out into the colosseums to be publicly executed in the trappings of an elaborate game.

But even if some of those slated for death were mass murderers, most today would have a problem with using their execution as a source of amusement. If someone were to take a modern-day killer on death row and throw him in the ring with a lion, there would most certainly be a public outcry against it. For example, the US Constitution has built in safeguards against cruel and unusual punishment. In the days of the Roman games, however, there was no such thing.

If you were condemned by the government of ancient Rome, your life was forfeit, and the state could do anything it wanted with it. In some instances, prisoners were even forced to act as mythological characters before being cruelly snuffed out in the final scene. Just imagine someone forcing an inmate to play a character for a modern-day film only to have them killed at the end of production. For most of us, such a thing would seem unimaginably monstrous, yet it was considered standard fare in Rome.

Even if the Roman games did not involve direct combat, certain elements of cruelty were still in place. Chariot races, for example, forced drivers to compete on a track at high rates of speed, and the main draw for spectators was the last lap when the charioteers would try to literally drive each other off the road. Charioteers were often flung headlong from their chariots and were killed or terribly maimed as a result.

One of the only peaceful pastimes of the early Roman games was the presentation of exotic animals in the Circus Maximus. In the early days, just the sight of an elephant or a lion or two was enough to get the crowds excited. But eventually, bloodshed was required here as well. And so, large-scale hunting was demonstrated before the masses, and in time, complete beast matches were arranged. Wild beasts were made to fight each other, as well as hapless humans.

Roman spectators could watch a crocodile take on a lion one moment, then see a bull charge a defenseless prisoner the next. The Roman public is said to have had a compulsion for entertainment. So much so that the Roman poet Decimus Junius Juvenal, better known simply as Juvenal, famously declared that "bread and circuses" were all that was needed in order for the Roman populace to remain content.

Juvenal proclaimed this in bitter sarcasm at the state that Rome had found itself in. He, like many of his contemporaries, felt that Romans had become so blinded by their need for entertainment that they had developed a complete disregard for their civic duties as citizens.

This callous disregard for the feelings of others, even the feelings of the condemned, stands in stark contrast to today's much more sensitive stance on both human and animal rights. Today, neither a bad crook nor a big cat would be sacrificed for the sake of the public. Such things would be considered incredibly cruel. So, having said that, the question remains—why didn't it seem that way for the Romans? Were the Romans just exceptionally cruel?

Considering what the Roman games came to consist of, it would be hard to argue anything different. But, of course, there is often more to a story than first meets the eye. So, let's examine the full history of the

Roman games to gain a better understanding of what may have motivated ancient Rome to routinely host these incredible spectacles.

Chapter 1 – Where Did the Games Begin?

"It was the wont of the immortal gods sometimes to grant prosperity and long impunity to men whose crimes they were minded to punish in order that a complete reverse of fortune might make them suffer more bitterly."

-Julius Caesar

Although there isn't a clear starting point as to when what we call the Roman games began, the practice is generally believed to have evolved from various religious festivities. Grand religious extravaganzas that celebrated Roman deities and religious rituals were indeed at the heart of the early Roman games. It became standard fare to have the public participate in games and activities sanctioned by the Roman state that were meant to foster solidarity while seeking divine blessings for continued prosperity.

The games followed a well-regulated routine in which everyone knew their part and moved in procession to celebrate Roman religion and culture. It is believed that the very first instance of the official Roman games—that is, when they were observed as an annual event—

may have occurred as far back as 366 BCE at a festival held in honor of the Roman god Jupiter.

However, more sporadic celebrations may date all the way back to a man named Lucius Tarquinius Priscus—the fifth king of Rome. Tarquinius's rule of Rome began in 616 BCE and ended in 579 BCE. This was long before the Roman Empire and even before the founding of the Roman Republic. It was from this basic city-state of Rome that the very first Roman games can be traced.

These festivals became known as the Ludi Romani, which literally translates into the "Roman Games." The festivals lasted for several days at a time. The events often consisted of the following formula: a parade, ritual sacrifices, and then finally, the Ludi Romani, or as we like to call them, the "Roman Games." During the pomp and circumstance of the parade portion of the festivities, observers were reminded in an elaborate fashion of the power of Rome and what Roman society expected of them as citizens.

And in order to magnify this feeling of obedience and civic duty, the parade followed predictable, highly orchestrated patterns, with participants put in place according to their rank or importance and with the significance of individual members being conveyed by the costumes they wore. On cue, these participants sang and gave oratory to commemorate important aspects of Roman religion, politics, and tradition.

Sacrificial animals often marched in the parade, and their distinction was also often designated by the wearing of ceremonial flowery garlands or special bows and ribbons tied around them. This was done to distinguish special ritual animals from regular pack animals, as well as to create the perception that these beasts of burden were voluntarily allowing themselves the honor of being made a sacrifice.

Obviously, animals do not have the wherewithal to make such decisions on their own, but the fact that a well-fed calf was decked out in garlands, wreaths, and bows sure made it seem like it was happily marching off to slaughter. The parade of the Ludi Romani was always followed by an official sacrifice of ritual animals. Like many ancient peoples, ancient Roman religion centered around the sacrifice of animals.

The custom of sacrificing a prized animal to a deity was meant to convey the sense of humanity giving up something it could have used for itself to their god. It's not that the gods needed a fatted calf, but rather, it represents the notion that a human being would be willing to give up—*to sacrifice*—something that they needed as a gift to the gods.

In exchange for this sacrifice, it was hoped that the gods would look favorably upon human beings, ensuring that they were healthy, protected, and well cared for. In the order of events at such a Roman festival, after the sacrifices were made, priests would then specifically pray for the gods to help meet the needs of the community. On some occasions, Roman priests might even take individual prayer requests.

Although pagan in its backdrop, such things are not all that different from Christian prayer requests for church members. In church, Christians often mention requests for prayer in the belief that the power of the unified faith of the church members would help to pull them through their difficult times. Romans did very much the same thing. And it was only after the sacrifices were complete and the prayers had been made that the Roman games would officially begin.

The early Roman games were more akin to their immediate predecessors in Greece. Yes, many of the traditions of Greece eventually found their way to Rome. It's for this reason that Roman civilization is often referred to as Greco-Roman, as the two cultures are intricately linked together. And in the early days of the Roman games, Greek influence is very evident. At the inception of the Ludi Romani, the main focus was on games of athletic skill and endurance, similar to the Olympic Games in Greece.

There were also games involving music, as well as theater, the latter of which was most definitely imported from Greece. The Romans, of course, would later put their own spin on these things by having condemned prisoners fight to the death. Perhaps even more disturbingly, the Romans would have the condemned act as "mimes," having them mime the actions of famous figures from Greek tragedies, essentially turning them into the ancient world's equivalent of "snuff films."

Yes, it's one thing to act out a tragic play in which the main character pretends to be killed or pretends to commit suicide; it's a whole other thing to force the main character of a production to actually lose their life. And shockingly enough, that's what the Romans would eventually do. Indeed, all manner of horrid entertainments awaited those in attendance at the Roman games.

Initially, however, the Roman games were a much tamer affair in comparison to the lethal nature that they would one day adopt. Rather than throwing people to lions, the early Romans were more likely to simply display lions for curious spectators at their circuses. In the early days of the Roman games, the main draw was not gladiatorial combat, as would later be the case, but rather chariot races.

In these games, the winning charioteer could win fame and renown for their exploits on the Roman race track. They could also win a whole lot of money. Charioteers received regular pay for their services in addition to prize money. And depending on the situation, that prize money could bring in a fortune. If a charioteer played his cards right, he could end up being quite a wealthy man.

Roman writer Juvenal said as much in his epic *Satires*, comparing the net income of Roman lawyers with that of prize-winning charioteers. Juvenal remarked, "How about advocates then? Tell me the sum they extract from their work in court, those bulging bundles of briefs. They talk big enough...Yet if you check their incomes (real, not declared), you'll find that a hundred lawyers make only as much as Lacerta of the Reds." For those unfamiliar, Lacerta was a famous charioteer for the Romans "red team" of racers (teams consisted of reds, blues, greens, and whites).

There were also basic athletic forms of entertainment, such as foot racing, wrestling, and boxing. In these halcyon days of yore, the games were the playground of the people, where they could enjoy a mild-mannered spectacle in their downtime. The main shift in the early Ludi Romani and the later Roman games was an increasing emphasis on regional and other political leaders of the Roman state.

In the beginning, the festivals were primarily dedicated to the Roman gods, but as time progressed, the festivities were increasingly used to emphasize specific rulers and the governmental systems of the state. It was during these massive celebrations that Roman leaders found the best opportunity to convey their directives to the masses. It was for this reason that what was initially a religious festival took on the trappings of a political rally or military parade, the latter of which became important, as Rome's military generally used the parade portion of the Ludi Romani to showcase their latest triumphs against neighboring rivals. It was quite common for the spoils of war to be held high in glorious triumph by Roman soldiers as they marched in lockstep during the elaborate procession. Even the famed Roman general Scipio Africanus, for example, first displayed his prowess before the early Roman Republic during one of the Roman games held in 213 BCE. Scipio would hold much grander games several years later in 206 BCE in commemoration of his victories he helped score in the Second Punic War.

Over time, three distinct types of Roman games began to emerge. First of all, there were the more standard games, which were controlled and organized by a civic magistrate known as an aedile. One of the most famous of these so-called aediles was the Roman historian and politician Cicero, who masterfully organized several Roman games.

The more excessive Roman games, which typically featured a special military triumph over one of Rome's enemies, were typically held by Rome's elite class of leaders. The top echelon of Rome's hierarchy was also responsible for the establishment of gladiatorial games, which pitted men against each other in what was often more or less mortal combat. It was the latter that quickly gained in popularity for a variety of reasons, with the most obvious reason being the general public's fascination with the spectacle of watching scenes of bloody combat. Such things might be shocking for us today, but for the ancient Romans, it was their equivalent of watching a football game. These blood sports developed into a profitable attraction with a high turnout.

Seizing on its popularity, the Roman elite began to host gladiatorial combat in commemoration of events. Even funerals were sometimes commemorated by the hosting of gladiatorial combat in the arena. Not very many of us today would commemorate our loved one's passing by going to watch a wrestling match, but for the ancient Romans, rather than sitting down to eat a meal with mourners, they just as well might sit in the arena to watch gladiators. This funerary practice was actually borrowed by the Romans from the Etruscans.

The Etruscans lived in northwestern Italy prior to their annexation by Rome and had borrowed much of their culture from the Greeks. The Etruscans valued athletic games just like the Greeks, but it was their habit of having elaborate "funeral games," in which gladiators competed against each other in memory of those who had passed, that really caught the attention of the Romans.

Early Christian writer Tertullian, who, due to his Christian faith, quite understandably condemned the practice, stated that before gladiatorial games were in vogue, there was a practice already in place of occasional human sacrifice. This was due to a belief among the masses that the "souls of the dead are propitiated by human blood." If the sacrifice of another person was believed to satisfy restless spirits, it really begs the question of who was going to satisfy the restless spirits of those who were sacrificed.

At any rate, as Tertullian put it, "The ancients thought they were performing a duty to the dead by this sort of spectacle after they had tempered its character by a more refined form of cruelty. For in time long past, in accordance with the belief that the souls of the dead are propagated by human blood, they used to purchase captives or slaves of inferior ability and to sacrifice them at funerals. Afterwards, they preferred to disguise this impiety by making it a pleasure. Thus, they found consolation for death in murder. Such is the origin of gladiatorial contest."

As Tertullian explains it, the gladiatorial games were used as an elaborate mask of what would otherwise have been viewed as cold-blooded murder. Just like the fatted calf dressed up in wreaths, garlands, and bows, the gladiators, dressed up in armors, helmets, and shields, were a distraction from their true purpose as a sacrificial lamb for the recently deceased.

Having said that, it was Scipio's grand gladiatorial games of 206 that perhaps demonstrated this practice best. These games were not only held in commemoration of the recent victories against Carthage but also in remembrance of both Scipio's father and uncle who had recently passed. Roman historian Livy captured Scipio's dramatic festivities quite well.

Livy tells us, "Scipio returned to [New] Carthage to pay his vows to the gods and to conduct the gladiatorial show which he had prepared in honor of his deceased father and uncle. The exhibition of gladiators was not made up from the class of men which lanistae are in the habit of pitting against each other, that is slaves sold on the platform and free men who are ready to sell their lives. In every case the service of the men who fought was voluntary and without compensation."

Livy made mention of *lanistae*, which was a kind of team owner who made it his business to buy, sell, trade, and train gladiators in the hopes of reaping considerable profits from their matches. Under the guidance of the *lanistae*, many of these gladiators were placed in special teams or "troupes," which were termed *familia gladiatorum*. This was basically a family of gladiators, who were prepped and primed to make as much profit for the *lanistae* as possible.

The Roman historian then went on to state, "In addition to this gladiatorial show there were funeral games so far as the resources of the province and camp equipment permitted." While the actual start date of the Roman games may be a bit murky, they seem to be intrinsically tied to Roman religion and views on the afterlife. The Romans, it seems, very much enjoyed a good show, and they were under the impression that the dearly departed would like one as well.

Chapter 2 – Political and Religious Implications of the Games

"Be prepared, when you speak before an assembly of men, to study their tastes, not, of course, everywhere and by every means, yet occasionally and to some extent. And when you do so, remind yourself that you are but doing the same as you do when, at the people's request, you honor or enfranchise those who have slain beasts manfully in the arena; even though they are murderers or condemned for some crime, you release them at the people's request. Everywhere then the people dominate and prevail."

-Roman orator, Marcus Cornelius Fronto

An indisputable aspect of the Roman games was the fact that they eventually came to fuse both religion and politics. And this fusion was often exported to client states of Rome when it was deemed desirable to put on a full demonstration of the "Roman brand," if you will. This was precisely the case in 168 BCE when the last of the long line of kings in Macedonia—King Perseus—was defeated.

In the wake of the Roman administrative takeover of Macedonia, Roman authorities wished to project not just Roman military might but also Roman political power, and this was often done through the extravagant spectacle of the Roman games. Roman General Lucius Aemilius Paulus Macedonicus was on the scene, and he staged Roman games at the Macedonian city of Amphipolis in order to demonstrate to the Macedonians just how cultured their conquerors were.

Roman historian Livy documented this moment of excess, writing, "The serious business was followed by an entertainment, a most elaborate affair staged at Amphipolis. This had been under preparation for a considerable time, and Paulus had sent messengers to the cities and kings of Asia to give notice of the event, while he had announced it in person to the leading citizens in the course of the Greek states. A large number of skilled performers of all kinds in the sphere of entertainment assembled from all over the world, besides athletes and famous horses, and official representatives with sacrificial victims; and all the other usual ingredients of the great games of Greece, provided for the sake of gods and men, were supplied on such a scale as to excite admiration not merely for the splendor of the display but also for the well-organized showmanship in a field where the Romans were at that time mere beginners."

Livy then goes on to state, "Banquets for the official delegations were put on, equally sumptuous and arranged with equal care. A remark of Paulus himself was commonly quoted, to the effect that a man who knew how to conquer in war was also a man who would know how to arrange a banquet and to organize a show." Yes, the Romans of those days were eager to show their subjected people that they really knew how to put on "a show."

And other regional kings did indeed take notice. The infamous Greek ruler of Syria—Antiochus IV Epiphanes—for one, began to introduce his own version of the Roman games at home. Perhaps even more infamously, Antiochus tried to enforce his own version of the games on the Jews of Judea, whom he had been attempting to subjugate. This led to the Maccabean revolt that overthrew the forces of Antiochus, and Antiochus himself died shortly thereafter in 164 BCE.

This event, which is recorded in the apocryphal First and Second Books of Maccabees, left a lasting impression on the Jewish people. Antiochus, in his lust for Hellenistic-styled games, tried to shove Greco-Roman culture down the Jews' throats—in some cases quite literally since there are accounts of Jews being force-fed pork. In his ruthless belligerence, he even went as far as to have his troops storm into the Jewish temple and sacrifice a pig on the sacred altar. This event would become known as the "abomination of desolation," and it would be mentioned by Jesus himself in the New Testament in both remembrance and as a foreshadowing of potential ill omens to come.

Antiochus IV Epiphanes's attempt to force the Jewish people into Greco-Roman gameplay was ultimately defeated by the Jewish Maccabean revolt, and the holiday of Hannukah was established in remembrance of the event. At any rate, by the 1st century BCE, powerful Romans, such as Roman General Pompey and Roman statesman Julius Caesar, used the Roman games to enhance their own image and standing.

As early as 73 BCE, a young statesman named Julius Caesar was attempting to impress his political rivals by putting on elaborate gladiatorial games. Caesar apparently outdid himself, however, and unleashed the backlash of an alarmed Roman Senate. As the Roman historian Suetonius put it, Caesar had "collected so immense a troop of combatants that his terrified political opponents rushed a bill through the House, limiting the number that anyone might keep in Rome; consequently, far fewer pairs fought than had been advertised."

Suetonius also gives us a vivid description of just how elaborate the Roman games under Caesar could be. At one point, he says, "His [Caesar's] public shows were of great variety. They included a gladiatorial contest, stage-plays for every Roman ward performed in several languages, chariot-races in the Circus, athletic competitions, and a mock naval battle."

Suetonius then goes on to reveal some of the political implications, mentioning, "At the gladiatorial contest in the Forum, a man named Furius Leptinus, of praetorian family, fought Quintus Calpenus, a barrister and former senator, to the death." He fought a former senator to the death? Just imagine a feat like this carried out among some of the political hacks of today!

Caesar's eventual rival, Pompey, in the meantime, used the games to commemorate everything from military conquests to the opening of theaters. This was the case in 55 BCE, which was documented by the Roman statesman Cicero. In a letter to an associate, Cicero spoke of the event. "To be sure, the show (if you are interested) was on the most lavish scale; but it would have been little to your taste, to judge by my own. To begin with, certain performers honored the occasion by returning to the boards, from which I thought they had honored their reputation by retiring. I need not give you further details—you know the other shows. "

Cicero then went on to say, "They did not even have the sprightliness which one mostly finds in ordinary shows—one lost all sense of gaiety in watching the elaborate productions. These I don't doubt you are very well content to have missed. What pleasure is there in getting a Clytemnestra with six hundred mules or a Trojan Horse with three thousand mixing bowls or a variegated display of cavalry and infantry equipment in some battle or other? The public gaped at all this; it would not have amused you at all. Or perhaps having scorned gladiators, you are sorry not to have seen the athletes!"

Cicero then acknowledges, "Pompey himself admits that they were a waste of time and midday oil! That leaves the venationes, two every day for five days, magnificent—nobody says otherwise. But what pleasure can a cultivated man get out of seeing a weak human being torn to pieces by a powerful animal or a splendid animal transfixed by a hunting spear? Anyhow, if these sights are worth seeing, you have seen them often; and we spectators saw nothing new."

Cicero mentions the *venationes*, or skilled hunters, who were sent out to hunt wild animals in the arena. While these kinds of spectacles certainly did draw crowds, many event managers, including the great Pompey himself, held a dismal view of them. You can even see Cicero's negative viewpoint of them in the above passage. Many considered them to be a "waste of time."

Julius Caesar was a man intricately linked to Pompey, both through the elite power circles in which they operated and through their own personal families. Caesar's daughter Julia, you see, had been joined in marriage to the general. Tragically, Julia passed away of sudden illness. Upon her death, Julius Caesar oversaw public festivities that included a banquet, games, and even a gladiatorial show for the masses who attended.

Such extravagance was simply part of the routine for prominent Roman figures such as Pompey and Caesar. But as one might imagine, holding these lavish and complicated extravaganzas wasn't cheap. They cost their hosts quite a bit of money. And the fact that one couldn't get much traction in the Roman political world without the ability to host these lavish games made it increasingly difficult for the less affluent to gain a foothold in Roman politics.

Cicero notes as much when recalling the political campaign of one Titus Annius Milo. Milo was attempting to become a Roman consul, but according to Cicero, he spent a fortune simply trying to hold more elaborate Roman games than his opponents had. In 52 BCE, Milo's campaign ended in scandal, and he was put on trial for the murder of his political rival, Publius Clodius Pulcher, during which he became Cicero's very own client. Milo was ultimately exiled for his actions, yet the public would long remember his generous extravagance in hosting public games and festivities.

Another Roman politician, one Publius Sestius, gained notoriety in relation to the Roman games under very different circumstances. For, in 56 BCE, Sestius had been hit with a charge of "irregular campaigning tactics." Part of this "irregular campaigning" apparently involved the utilization of his own personal goon squad of gladiators, which was used as hired enforcers while he was in office as a tribune. Another famous political scandal of the 1ˢᵗ century BCE involving the Roman games occurred in 62 BCE when Lucius Licinius Murena was accused of bribery when he supposedly attempted to swap expensive seats in the arena in exchange for political benefits.

The previous year, Cicero himself had attempted to codify into Roman law a prohibition on using the Roman games as a perk when campaigning. This bit of lawmaking stipulated that those actively campaigning for public positions should not be allowed to host any games to prevent candidates from using the games to curry political favor. Yet, the Roman games and, in particular, the cobbling together of gladiators as personal guards continued to be the norm during political campaigns.

And the games would continue after the Roman Republic transitioned into the Roman Empire. According to writer and historian Roland Auguet, the very first Roman emperor, Emperor Augustus, was known to have as many as "625 pairs of gladiators for each spectacle." Needless to say, that was an awful lot of gladiators, and it made for quite an elaborate and ostentatious display.

These displays were meant to convey Roman power to both the average Roman citizen and any foreign visitors who just happened to be in Rome at the time. Under Augustus, the events were streamlined even further, with special efforts made to assign seating to different segments of Roman society. Roman soldiers sat in one section, the commoners in another, and, of course, the upper crust had seats of their own.

Augustus's successor Tiberius had an incredible disdain for the Roman games and felt that while it might have been fun for the plebeians (commoners) and other lower classes, it was well below his station as emperor. But although he didn't care too much for it, his sons, Germanicus and Drusus, did. This imperial father was still occasionally appalled, even by the passions that his own children had, for the games.

As the Roman historian Tacitus explained, "A gladiatorial display was given in the names of the Emperor's adopted son Germanicus and his own son Drusus. The latter was abnormally fond of bloodshed. Admittedly it was worthless blood, but the public was shocked and his father Tiberius was reported to have reprimanded him." It's interesting to note Tacitus's words, "worthless blood," which demonstrates the contempt that Romans had for the lower classes who performed in the games.

At any rate, Tacitus then went on to state, "The Emperor himself kept away. Various reasons were given—his dislike of crowds, or his natural glumness, or unwillingness to be compared with Augustus, who had cheerfully attended." It was Tiberius's disapproval of the games that often caused his subjects to seek out games elsewhere. This led to more underground venues popping up by the same lower classes that Tiberius seemed to so despise.

Sadly, the ramshackle arenas that were often created by amateurs led to terrible collapses. On one occasion, a man named Atilius had a wooden amphitheater built only for it to collapse and kill some fifty thousand people. It was tragedies such as this that led to Rome building one of its greatest architectural wonders—the Roman Colosseum.

By the time of the Colosseum, the Roman games were ritualized and infused with religious and political Roman imagery. When a gladiator perished, for example, a man dressed as Charon—the deity representing death—stepped forward and proceeded to hit the defeated gladiator's corpse with a mallet. This apparently signified death's grip on the fallen.

After this bit of theatrics, another man dressed as the Roman deity Mercury would poke the fallen gladiator with a red-hot iron. Along with the religious imagery this invoked, the striking of the fallen with a hammer and prodding with an iron were done just to make sure the defeated gladiator really was dead. If the gladiator didn't get up after being hit with a hammer and burned with an iron, it could be safely assumed that he was no longer among the living.

As the customs mentioned in this chapter well indicate, the Roman games became an intrinsic part of both religion and politics for the average Roman. They felt that their gods needed blood, and the gladiator was the sacrificial lamb to satiate them. The Romans also sought to use the game to project political and military power. He who could throw the most elaborate games was considered a real statesman. It was bread and circuses that made the Roman world go round.

Chapter 3 – The Gladiators of the Roman Games

"What beauty set Eppia on fire? What youth captured her? What did she see that made her endured being called a ludia [gladiator's woman]? For her darling Sergius had already begun to shave, and to hope for retirement due to a wounded arm. Moreover, there were many deformities on his face; for instance, there was a huge wart on the idle of his nose which was rubbed by his helmet, and a bitter matter dripped continually from one eye. But he was a gladiator: this makes them Hyancinthuses. She preferred this to her children and her country, that woman preferred this to her sister and her husband. The sword is what they love."

-Roman poet, Decimus Junius Juvenal

The notion of throwing two people into an arena to fight to the death first became popular in the Roman Republic sometime around 264 BCE. Gladiators were first used as a gruesome means to honor the dead, and gladiatorial combat was often done to honor the very rich dead since the average Roman could not afford such excess at their funerals. It was in that fateful year of 264 BCE that a noble Roman named Junius Brutus had his death commemorated by having enslaved men do battle against each other in what would become standard gladiatorial fashion.

These gladiators were not men who wanted to fight but rather men who were forced to fight. This first wave of gladiators in Rome was referred to as *bustuarii* (singular: *bustuarius*), which is a word related to death and the grave. The name seemed fitting since the gladiators first performed as part of the last rites ceremony to honor deceased Roman elites. In the early days, many of these memorial matches didn't occur in an arena or the Colosseum but rather took place in the "cattle market" or, as the Romans called it, the Forum Boarium.

It wasn't quite so glamorous to have gladiators duke it out at a cattle market, but the backdrop of a forum for such an event set the general standard of things to come. In these early days of Roman gladiatorial games, there were no stands in which spectators could sit. Instead, they simply gathered around in the background, claiming whatever spot they could find to watch the match. Just imagine regal Romans after a funeral procession standing on the sidelines of one of these bloody events, supposedly carried out in honor of the dearly departed.

The closeness of the spectators to the fighters created an intimate, if disturbing, connection. During these games, the gladiators typically battled in pairs and were outfitted with the same minimal armor, small shield, and short sword, known as a *gladius*. The fighters began the match in single pairs, but this number could multiply as the match progressed. In some cases, there could be as many as one hundred gladiators locked in combat at one time.

Gladiatorial fighting after funerals was also often accompanied by a banquet. It probably seems rather sinister to the modern reader to imagine the ancients literally wining and dining themselves after watching a gladiatorial bloodbath, but this was apparently the custom. As indicated, rather than the Roman gladiatorial games being an event held in the middle of an arena with thousands of fans in attendance, gladiatorial fighting was initially viewed as being part of the last rites of the deceased.

Some have suggested that this Roman concept of gladiators—which was borrowed from the Etruscans—also stems from an older Roman tradition of committing human sacrifice over the graves of the deceased. If true, the smokescreen of gladiatorial combat was simply a dressed-up form of the same habit of human sacrifice. Roman writer Festus seemed to confirm this when he remarked, "It was the custom, to sacrifice prisoners on the tombs of valorous warriors; when the cruelty of this custom became evident, it was decided to make gladiators fight before the tomb."

As Festus seems to indicate, gladiators were an offshoot of an older tradition, and they had simply been given a facelift for more modern Roman sensibilities. Rather than simply tying up a hapless victim at a stone idol or before a funeral pyre, they would force two men to fight to the death instead. If true, either way, the end result of spilled blood as a sacrifice for the recently departed remained in force.

The ancient Romans believed that the spirits of their dead required certain rites to be conducted, and if they were not, they feared that the ghosts of these dead men just might come back from the grave and haunt them. It might sound absolutely ridiculous to us today, but this was a real concern for the ancient Romans. And the spilled blood of gladiators as a sacrifice for the supposed appeasement of restless spirits was still part of Roman funeral customs in the days of the Roman Republic.

Christian writer and apologist Tertullian would easily make this very connection in the 2nd century CE when he wrote, "The ancients thought that performing this spectacle was a duty to the dead, after they tempered it with a more humane atrocity. For, once upon a time, since it had been believed that the souls of the dead were propitiated by human blood, having purchased captives or slaves of bad character, they sacrificed them as part of funeral ritual."

Tertullian then went on to explain, "Later they decided to mask the impiety as entertainment. And so those they had purchased and trained in what arms and in whatever way they could, only that they might learn to be killed, they soon exposed to death on the appointed day of the funeral. Thus, they sought consolation for death in homicide. This was the origin of the munus." *Munus* is a word that means "obligation," as in the obligatory duty to have gladiators perform at a funeral.

The games would become much more elaborate over time, of course, and most especially as it pertained to gladiators. The gladiatorial fighters evolved into set categories of warriors. Although the fighters may have hailed from all over the empire, they were usually forced to act out the part of specific stereotypical caricatures of Roman adversaries. There were four basic types of gladiators—the Samnites, the Myrmillo, the Retiarius, and the Thraex.

Those who were selected to represent the Thraex group were outfitted in traditional weapons and armor used by the warriors of old who hailed from the region of Thrace in the Balkans. The gladiator playing the role of a Thraex wore the infamous high-crested helmet of a Thracian, which would come to symbolize gladiators as a whole. Thraex fighters were also equipped with a small square shield, greaves to protect their arms, and a short, curved dagger with which to attack their opponents.

The games created special strategies for the gladiators involved since each category of fighter had its own strengths and weaknesses due to the weapons and armor with which the gladiators were equipped. Although a Thraex gladiator was nimble and fierce with their dagger, they could be captured with a carefully aimed net by an opponent. That iconic, high-crested helmet, in fact, was quite easily snagged by the nets wielded by the Retiarii gladiators.

The Retiarii were known as the "fishermen" because these lightly armored fighters carried fishing-styled nets, as well as a three-pronged trident. These gladiators were highly effective against Thraex fighters.

Other gladiators, however, who wore smooth, low-crested helmets to which nets were unable to attach, were a different story. Some helmets also had narrow visors, which the trident-hurling Retiarii were unable to penetrate. Different helmets might allow better vision while also rendering the head more vulnerable.

Another gladiator variation to appear later during the Roman games was the so-called "Secutor," who were heavily armored and wore a "bullet-shaped" helmet, the latter of which would be the favorite of Roman Emperor (and part-time gladiator) Commodus. Some other forms of gladiators have been discovered that seem to be much rarer. According to writer and historian Roland Auguet, there is an unknown variant that was later discovered by archaeologists who happened upon two separate bas-reliefs memorializing gladiatorial combat that depict the same unknown category of fighter.

In these depictions, the gladiator is paired with a Retiarius and seems to be equipped to do battle with the Retiarius's net. The character has a special cone-like contraption on his arm, with a rod protruding out of it, topped off with a hook. It seems that this hook was used by the gladiator to snatch up and rip away the net wielded by the Retiarius. At the end of the day, every aspect of a gladiator's dress had its strengths and weaknesses, and it was up to the gladiators who fought each other to make the best of both.

One of the most interesting aspects of these games was how well versed and interactive the spectators were with the battling gladiators. If fans found themselves close enough to the action, they would proceed to shout directives from the stands. Just like a modern-day fan at a basketball game shouting at a player to make a basket or pass the ball off to another player, Roman spectators shouted out completely unsolicited advice to the gladiators below.

It was entirely up to the gladiator whether they heeded such advice, however, and in the heat of the battle, it's likely little attention was being paid to a bunch of loud-mouthed fans. But if the gladiator ended up on the losing end and was bested by his opponent, they couldn't help but notice. For it was the fans up in the stands who played a role in a defeated gladiator's fate.

If the spectators felt that the gladiator had fought bravely, they could be moved to call for them to be spared. The means with which they did this is debated, although it is popularly believed that the sign from fans to spare a gladiator was a thumbs up, whereas the signal for them to be killed was the infamous thumbs down. For the sake of speculation, let's stick with the most common perception. Thumbs up, the gladiator lives, and thumbs down, he dies.

It wasn't the spectators who ultimately decided the fate of the gladiator, though; that decision belonged to the so-called "editor" of the Roman games. The editor was the one who orchestrated the whole series of games and oversaw how they were carried out. Much of the time, the editor was actually the Roman emperor or some other high-up official. But even though the editor was the one who ultimately made the decision, they almost always followed the whims of the public.

Let's just imagine for a moment that the crowd is ready to signal with a thumbs down, meaning they wish for a defeated gladiator to be killed. Now picture the gladiator defeated, his opponent standing over him with his sword in hand. This man's life is now in the hands of the audience and the editor. Almost immediately, the crowd shouts, "Finish him!" and soon, nearly everyone in the audience presents an outstretched hand with their thumb pointed down.

The editor, in the meantime, watches all of this very carefully, and not willing to go against the wishes of the crowd, he stands up and dramatically turns his own thumb down as well. The victorious gladiator below sees this cue and immediately slits his defeated opponent's throat, thereby ending his life. This was typically how gladiators met their end. If the audience, however, felt that the gladiator showed spirit and fought well, they just might call for him to be spared, causing the editor to rule likewise.

Interestingly enough, the more years one remained a gladiator, the greater the chances were of survival. You see, whereas veteran gladiators may have developed a solid fan base, it was the new gladiators who faced the most hostile audiences. If a gladiator was well known and had developed a reputation as being a good and honorable fighter, the audience was more likely to demand that they be spared so that their beloved gladiator could be seen performing again in future games.

If, however, after everything was said and done and the audience and editor ruled that the gladiator was to die, the defeated fighter was expected to stoically accept their fate. As part of their training, it was always drilled into the gladiator's mind to face death as bravely as they had fought for life. In defeat, they were trained to not struggle and simply wait for the final blow from their opponent.

And incredibly enough, it seems that most gladiators did just that. These warriors, for the most part, accepted the hand that fate had dealt them and stretched out their necks to make it easier for their assailant to cut. This was the final curtain call for many gladiators in the Roman games.

As bad as it might seem, in some ways, perhaps those who died early on in their career were better off. Those gladiators who continued to fight and survive certainly didn't have a very good go of it. The Roman physician Galen gives us a startling window into what the life of a veteran gladiator was like.

After several years of fighting in the ring, it shouldn't be too surprising that these men would develop all manner of physical and mental ailments by the time that they got out. Galen took note of these deficiencies and even seemed to diagnose something that persistently plagued these veteran gladiators. This diagnosis would be similar to the modern-day diagnosis of "PTSD" (post-traumatic stress disorder). As Galen describes to us, "In the amassing of [the athletes'] great quantity of flesh and blood their mind is lost in the vast mire. Receiving no stimulation to develop, it remains as stupid as that of brutes...They fatigue themselves to the limit and then gourmandize to excess, prolonging their repast often into the middle of the night."

Galen then goes on to state, "Analogous rules to those guiding their exercise and eating regulate also their sleep. At the hour when people who live according to the laws of nature quit work to take their lunch, the athletes are rising...While athletes pursue their profession, their body remains in this dangerous state [of hyper development]. When they quit it, they fall into a state even more dangerous."

The state that we might call PTSD is what Galen refers to as a "dangerous state" of alertness. The gladiator is accustomed to a life of adrenaline, yet when they suddenly stop and try to break away from this life of blood-rushing adrenaline, they find themselves a nervous wreck.

As Galen puts it, "Some [gladiators] die shortly after, others live a little longer, but never reach old age...Their bodies enfeebled by the jolts they have received, [they] are predisposed to become sick on the least provocation. Their eyes, ordinarily sunken, readily become the seat of fluxions; their teeth, so readily injured, fall out. With muscles and tendons frequently torn, their articulations become incapable of resisting strain and readily dislocate. From the standpoint of health, no condition is more wretched."

After coming to this determination, Galen then warns, "Many who have been perfectly proportioned fall into the hands of trainers who develop them beyond measure, overload them with flesh and blood, and make them just the opposite...[Fighters] develop a disfigured countenance hideous to look upon. Limbs broken or dislocated and eyes gouged out of sockets show the kind of beauty produced. These are the fruits they gather. When they no longer exercise their profession, they lose sensation, their limbs become dislocated, and, as I have said, they become completely deformed."

In other words, after a life serving in the Roman games came to an end, the wrecked shell of a human being would find themselves entirely unable to live a normal life. They had become used to being under the spotlight and glare of the arena, violently living for the moment. How in the world would someone who had been subjected to such intense conditions suddenly pack everything up and live a quiet life on a farm?

Yet, this is indeed apparently what some gladiators did. Although it surely must have been a struggle, some successful gladiators managed to retire and use the money they earned to retire in peace. But after the trauma a gladiator had been subjected to, just how peaceful their retirement might have been is anyone's guess.

Chapter 4 – Spartacus Fights for Freedom

"He's young still, physically fit to bear arms, and hot-blooded. Gossip claims that with no official compulsion, but no ban either, he'll sign his freedom away to some tyrant of a lanista, take the gladiator's oath... They'll hock the family plate, or pledge poor Mummy's portrait, and spend their last fiver to add relish to their gourmet earthenware: thus they're reduced to the gladiators' mess-stew."

-Roman poet, Decimus Junius Juvenal

The most famous participant of the Roman games to come down to us through history is, without a doubt, a gladiator known simply as Spartacus. Spartacus hailed from a little-known place called Thrace. The ancient region of Thrace comprised sections of Greece, Turkey, and Bulgaria. As it was a rich agricultural area, the Thracians were initially known as farmers.

As time passed, however, inner turmoil among the Thracians began to develop. Petty factions and rivalries led to constant infighting that managed to weaken the Thracian state. Neighboring nations took notice and used the vulnerability of Thrace to literally enslave its people. Greece lorded over the Thracians by the 7th century BCE before the Persian Empire rose in the east and swept the Thracians into their orbit.

Despite the fact they were a conquered people, the Thracians had retained a reputation for being fearsome fighters. Even under Persian dominion, they were widely used as mercenaries to field Persian armies. The Persian Empire soon went into decline, however, and its borders retreated beyond the land of Thrace. Left to their own machinations, for a time, the Thracians forged their own kingdom.

But it was short lived. In 335 BCE, the armies of a Macedonian king named Alexander the Great decimated what was left of Thracian independence and brought the region firmly under Macedonian control. The situation for Thrace then changed once again in 169 BCE when Thrace, as well as Macedonia itself, was absorbed into the Roman Republic. Despite the shifting political powers that ruled over them, Thracians still had a vibrant culture of their own.

And their martial abilities as fighters were still in demand. So much so that Romans were quick to pick up on it. Soon, Thracians were being imported into Roman arenas to perform as gladiators in the Roman games. The man named Spartacus, of course, would become one of the most famous of these warriors. It seems that Spartacus began his career as a mercenary and fought in the ranks of the Roman army. It was indeed quite common for Thracians like Spartacus to serve in Rome's so-called "auxiliary troop" detachments.

Although the details are a bit murky, it seems that Spartacus eventually grew weary of the life of a Roman soldier and decided to go AWOL (absent without official leave). Abandoning a military post always has severe consequences, and this was especially the case for the Romans, who viewed such negligence as being treacherous and beyond the pale. Most of the time, those who abandoned their assignments were killed right on the spot if they were unlucky enough to be tracked down by the Romans.

Spartacus apparently realized that his actions had made him persona non grata among the Romans. And knowing that he was now an enemy of Rome, he made the best of it, joining homegrown resistance efforts against the Roman occupiers. He knew that the Romans were coming for him eventually, so he figured that he would at least go down fighting.

But Spartacus did not die on the battlefield against Rome (at least not this early in his life); instead, he was captured by his former Roman taskmasters. The big question, which historians haven't quite figured out, is why such a rabble-rouser wasn't simply killed outright for his trespasses against Rome. Could it be that he was such a daring and bold fighter that he impressed the Romans enough to spare his life? Whatever the case may be, he was soon taken captive, and once the Romans connected to the gladiatorial games took one look at this tough Thracian, it was determined that he would make a great addition to the arena.

Now a man forced into slavery, Spartacus would be a forced participant of the Roman games. He began his career under the auspices of one Gnaeus Cornelius Lentulus Batiatus. Lentulus Batiatus was in charge of a gladiatorial training center in Capua, Italy. During the course of his training, Spartacus, like all other gladiators, was carefully guarded and monitored. All he was allowed to do was eat, sleep, and train while being under constant surveillance and the threat of death should he defy his captors.

The gladiators were locked up in stalls, little better than what one might expect an animal to be held in. They were heavily guarded and only allowed out to train or to be led to the arena. Being a gladiator was a brutal business, and most tossed into the ring would have a short lifespan. Even if matches were not always lethal in outcome, the likelihood of sustaining severe injuries was extraordinarily high.

The fact that Spartacus lasted as long as he did bears testament to just how good of a fighter he really was. Spartacus was such a good gladiator that it was the person who was unfortunate enough to be matched against him who would face terrible repercussions. No doubt many men died by Spartacus's hand. Most didn't want to have to fight in the ring like this, but they had no choice.

All gladiators, when the time came, were forced out of the stockades that held them and made to burst forth into the arena so that these vicious Roman games could begin. If a gladiator was a little too slow to emerge, one of their handlers would be there ready and waiting to hit them with a whip or prod them forward with a flaming torch. These gladiators usually did not wish to do battle with one another but rather were forced to do their handlers' bidding.

Nevertheless, even under these brutal conditions, Spartacus began to get to know some of his fellow gladiators. And after the roar of the crowd had ceased and Spartacus and those who had survived that day's events were herded back into their living quarters, they would converse with each other. It was during these private moments that he and his fellow gladiatorial peers of the Roman games began to plot their escape.

It's not entirely clear how Spartacus and his comrades broke out of their confinement, but it's known that once they did, they made a beeline for the mess hall where their food was usually prepared. They didn't do so because they were hungry and needed a snack, mind you; they simply knew the kitchen was a place they could grab knives and other implements with which to defend themselves.

You see, when the gladiators were not battling it out in the arena, they were denied access to weapons. Since these weapons were locked up and out of reach, the next best thing was to grab kitchen utensils that could be wielded as basic weapons. After this, they then proceeded to cut through the men who guarded them. Slashing and hacking their way out of the compound, the runaway gladiators were able to hide out in the wilderness while they planned their next move.

It took the leadership of that star gladiator of the Roman games—Spartacus—to hold the band of gladiators together. Shortly after Spartacus and his comrades escaped from their confines, their old taskmaster Lentulus Batiatus lodged a complaint with Roman authorities, resulting in an all-out manhunt for the renegades. Leading this charge was a Roman praetor by the name of Gaius Claudius Glaber.

Fortunately for Spartacus and his group, Rome's crack troops were way too busy fighting the various wars and insurrections that had recently erupted than to deal with a slave rebellion of gladiators. The Roman Republic had entered a period of tremendous upheaval and couldn't expend its best military resources just to take down a group of gladiators.

As such, Glaber was forced to put together a rather motley crew of his own, utilizing fresh recruits who were not the most experienced of fighters. Even though these men would be well armed, their lack of experience would be clearly evident upon facing off with the battle-hardened gladiators. Compounding Glaber's challenge of rounding up Spartacus and the other escaped gladiators was that Spartacus's rebellion had become a kind of movement that had gained steam with the enslaved masses of Rome. Soon, several other slaves from the surrounding area had escaped to join up with Spartacus's roving band.

These escapees that flocked to Spartacus were mostly domestic workers and field hands—not exactly skilled warriors ready for combat—but the fact that Spartacus's main group of gladiators was able to add auxiliary troops of any kind made the task of putting down what was initially a minor rebellion a much more difficult task. Spartacus had also created his own mountain fortress atop Mount Vesuvius, making it exceedingly difficult for any force to go on the offensive against him.

Initially, his pursuers attempted a war of attrition, thinking that they could starve the rebels down from their mountain stronghold. Glaber parked his forces around the mountain and simply waited for the gladiators to come down. This proved to be a big mistake since Spartacus and company, who were well versed in how to ambush their enemies, were able to launch a sneak attack in the middle of the night against the enemy camp.

They descended the mountain right in the midst of Glaber's forces and, catching them unaware, absolutely decimated them. Their opponents were forced to flee, and it seems that Praetor Glaber either perished in the struggle or simply gave up the fight, as his name is not brought up in association with Spartacus thereafter. The Roman enforcers, who were forced to flee, left behind food, armor, and other important supplies at the base of the mountain.

This proved to be a much-needed resource for the desperate gladiators, who quickly nourished their bodies with Roman rations and armed themselves with Roman armaments. Authorities in Rome were furious about what had happened at Mount Vesuvius, and unable to tolerate the notion that a ragtag group of gladiators would be able to best Roman power, it was arranged to have proper Roman legions—the best Roman troops available—to take on the renegades.

Despite the inclusion of the powerful legionaries, the first battle between these Roman troops and the rebels was a decisive failure for Rome. An entire detachment of troops was defeated. Spartacus then went on the offensive and led a portion of his fighters to assault another Roman legion nearby, and it, too, was defeated. With Roman legions smashed before them, Spartacus's gladiators were, at least for the time being, able to take to the countryside unopposed.

Before their oppressors could regroup, Spartacus took the initiative and attempted to put distance between himself and Rome. Roman troops were soon in hot pursuit, however, and the gladiators would have to often take to rearguard attacks to fend them off. The gladiators were fierce fighters, but the Roman soldiers were relentless, leading to several back-and-forth exchanges between the two.

Spartacus's large group of followers had become divided in the meantime, with one portion overseen by Spartacus himself and the other portion by a fellow gladiator and escapee of the Roman games named Crixus. In 72 BCE, the gladiator rebellion was struck a terrible blow when the forces manned by Crixus were defeated by a Roman legion.

Crixus was in command of tens of thousands of rebels at the time, but after the Roman legion tore through his ranks, he was only in command of a small fraction of that number. Spartacus was both enraged and alarmed at what had happened, knowing that it wouldn't be long before the hammer dropped on him as well. As such, he finally decided that it was time to take the battle to the Romans themselves.

A wealthy and noble Roman by the name of Marcus Licinius Crassus, in the meantime, took charge of the efforts of ridding the Roman Republic of the menace that Spartacus and his rebels posed. Spartacus's roving band, after all, was now regularly raiding Roman settlements for supplies, and such transgressions could not continue if the Roman Republic was to stand. Crassus led a resurgent Roman army against the rebels and steadily pushed them southward.

Reaching the coast of southern Italy, the group realized that they would have to find a means of passage across the waters lest they be driven into the sea. It was then that Spartacus concocted a scheme involving Cilician pirates (another brand of hunted outlaw) to ferry them to the island of Sicily. Here, Spartacus believed he could bolster his forces and prepare for a final showdown with Rome.

Spartacus was double-crossed by the pirates (apparently, you just can't trust pirates), for after taking an advance fee for transport from Spartacus, the pirates simply took the money and ran. This left Spartacus and his group stranded in southern Italy with no means of leaving the Italian Peninsula. With the forces of Rome closing in, out of sheer desperation, these escapees from the Roman games began to build makeshift crafts out of whatever wood they could find.

Little better than rafts, these treacherous vessels were now the only means of escaping certain death at the hands of a resurgent Roman army. This proved futile, however, since these makeshift crafts proved unable to tolerate the strong current of the four-mile strait that separated mainland southern Italy from Sicily. Cunning Crassus, in the meantime, had actually built a walled fortification zone spanning the entire forty-mile width of southern Italy, essentially locking the rebels in place. Now Crassus could simply starve the gladiators into submission without having to even fight them.

Spartacus wasn't willing to give up without a fight, though, and in 71 BCE, he sent his men smashing into the Roman fortifications. These tough gladiators actually scaled the walls and took the fight to the Romans. Utilizing their hard-honed skills and toughness learned during their stint in the Roman games, these warriors managed to overrun the walls that were built to keep them caged in, and once again, they made a mad dash to the north.

Hunted and hounded by the Romans, Spartacus and his remaining followers ended up making their last stand shortly thereafter. The Romans were able to make short work of the tired and weary gladiators, killing tens of thousands of them in one battle. Spartacus—that great champion of the Roman games—was among the number to have died that day.

Chapter 5 – Christians and the Roman Games

"Too mad with passion to defer or check his wrath, [the judge] appoints that they shall be burned with cruel fire. They, rejoicing, bid the throng not weep...By this time, they were entering a place enclosed by tiers of seats in a circle, where frenzied crowds attend and are drunk with much blood of wild beasts, when the din rises from the bloody shows, and as the gladiator, whose life is being held cheap, falls under the stroke of the stark sword there is a roar of delight."

-Roman poet, Aurelius Clemens Prudentius

The image of Christians being thrown to the lions at the Roman Colosseum seems to be seared into the memory of Western civilization. Christianity, a religion born in the Middle East, collided with Greco-Roman culture with explosive results. The first great persecution of the Christians of Rome occurred in 64 CE in the aftermath of the so-called "Great Fire" of Rome.

Historians still do not know for sure what happened, but for centuries, it has been widely believed that the depraved Nero set the fire himself, only to blame it on Christians. Even though no one can conclusively say that this is what happened, there are a lot of factors that make this scenario seem feasible.

The Roman emperor, it seems, had a strong—although entirely insidious—motive for setting Rome alight. Nero, as it turns out, wanted to demolish large parts of the city to make way for new construction. And after the fire leveled several structures to the ground, that is, in fact, exactly what he did.

Many have pointed to these events as an indication that the whole thing had been planned by Nero in the first place. But even if he hadn't, the Christians were a convenient group to blame these horrible crimes on. Even though today, it might be hard for us to understand it, the Romans felt that the Christians were the absolute worst of the worst.

For one thing, the average Roman grossly misunderstood the religion and believed that Christians were a part of a warped secret sect that practiced abominable things. For example, Romans commonly misunderstood the practice of communion, likening it to cannibalism. But why would they do this? It is because they misunderstood the words of Jesus that Christians quoted in regard to the practice of communion.

Just consider the Bible verses from Luke 22:19-20, which read, "And he took bread, gave thanks and broke it, and gave it to them, saying, 'This is my body given for you; do this in remembrance of me.' In the same way, after supper, he took the cup, saying, 'This cup is the new covenant in my blood, which is poured out for you.'"

For the average Roman who knew nothing of Christianity, hearing Christians quote such passages could be startling. Non-Christian Romans thought that Christians were actually commemorating the eating of Christ's body and the drinking of his blood. Today, we are fully aware of the symbolism involved, but back when Christians were an obscure sect, such things were easily misunderstood.

Furthermore, there were certainly those who did understand the symbolic nature but chose to exploit the confusion over it to make Christians look bad. For those that didn't like Christians, the easiest way to publicly shame them would be to point and shout, "Hey! Look over there! It's Christians! They're nothing but a bunch of cannibals!"

Christians were also believed to be weird because they frequently met in graveyards. Ironically, the main reason for Christians meeting in graveyards was due to the fact that they were so persecuted. The cemetery was simply a safe place to meet away from prying eyes. But one can only imagine that this habit only added to Christian strangeness.

Some of the more zealous followers, however, may very well have also preferred standing around graves due to the Christian belief that the dead would be resurrected in the last days. It was these more apocalyptic visions of Christianity that Nero and others latched onto after the Great Fire of Rome.

Christians continually spoke of how Rome and everything else would soon go up in flames, so it wasn't hard to claim that perhaps some Christian provocateurs set Rome on fire in an attempt to trigger the very Armageddon of which they spoke. Some modern historians, in fact, have since taken a good second look at the Great Fire of Rome and seriously considered the possibility that Nero was telling the truth after all and that the fire really was started by Christians.

But even if the fire was initially ignited by some misguided Christian or Christians, it certainly didn't give Nero the right to persecute every single Christian in the Roman Empire as punishment. Such a thing would be akin to punishing every single Muslim for 9/11 just because the hijackers happened to be Muslim. Obviously, today, we know that such collective punishments are wrong, but in Nero's day, they were fair game.

And so it was that massive numbers of Christians were crucified, thrown to the lions, and lit up as human torches, all to supposedly teach the members of this mysterious sect a lesson. At any rate, it was the Great Fire of Rome that would lead to the greatest construction the Roman Games would render—the Roman Colosseum.

Prior to the Colosseum, temporary wooden structures were used for the Roman games. Many of these were burned to a crisp in the Great Fire of Rome. Immediately after the devastation, the Roman public's desire for the Roman games was satiated once again through temporary structures, which were erected just for the purpose of the main event before being taken down.

It wasn't until Emperor Vespasian came to power in 69 CE that Rome began work on a permanent place to hold the Roman games. This grand structure, which was partially built with a large labor force of thousands of slaves and prisoners of war, would become known as the Roman Colosseum. It should be noted that many of those prisoners of war were taken from Jerusalem.

Jewish freedom fighters who had struggled with the Romans during the great siege that resulted in the destruction of their sacred temple in 70 CE ended up being forced to lay down stones for the Colosseum. The more cynical among us might be tempted to think that the whole assault on Judea in 70 CE—the very same year that construction on the Colosseum began—might not have been a coincidence. It is a fact that much of the funding for this construction project was achieved by way of the treasures stolen from the temple in Jerusalem. But could it also be that Rome saw a prime opportunity to create a massive slave labor force by attacking Judea? At any rate, it is rather chilling that Jewish prisoners of war, who were pulled from the wrecked rubble of their sacred temple, were forced to lay the stone foundations of the Roman Colosseum, in which so many of their descendants—both Jewish and Christian—would be persecuted.

According to Roman Jewish historian Josephus, just prior to Titus becoming emperor, he, as the general of the Roman army in Judea from 66 to 70 CE, made sure that many Jewish captives from the conflict in that region were brought back to Rome. Before the Colosseum was opened, several other Roman games were held by Titus in various locales, in which these captive Jews were forced to participate.

In fact, it is said that as many as 2,500 of these condemned prisoners of war died in just one Roman game. The inaugural games of the Colosseum, in the meantime, would be held in 80 CE during the last year of Titus's reign as emperor. But the Colosseum would not be fully operational until Emperor Domitian's reign in 81 CE.

Domitian was fascinated with grand architecture, and he would end up launching many feverish building projects during his reign. As the Roman historian Plutarch once wryly noted, Domitian seemed to be afflicted with "a disease of building and a desire, like Midas had, of turning everything to gold or stone."

It was Domitian who added the finishing touches of the hypogeum, which consisted of underground passageways in which animals and gladiators could be held until trap doors were opened, allowing them to walk out into the main stage of the arena. Just imagine Rome's religious and political dissidents helplessly huddled together in fear when a trap door was suddenly released, allowing several wild and hungry lions or a bloodthirsty group of gladiators to emerge.

Rome had a long history of throwing dissidents of all kinds into the arena. Anyone who disagreed with Roman rule, whether militarily or simply philosophically, ran the risk of being condemned to a grisly fate in the Colosseum. Ever since Judea (southern Israel) was incorporated into the Roman Empire, Jewish religious and political dissidents were frequent fodder for the Roman games.

The whole idea of feeding folks to lions was certainly not a new one for the Romans when the Colosseum was built. And at the very first inaugural games for the Roman Colosseum in 80 CE, among the main events was indeed a showing of *Damnatio ad bestias,* which is Latin for "condemnation to beasts." During this routine, the criminally condemned, whether the reason for their condemnation was theft, murder, or simply refusing to bow down to the emperor, were strategically placed in the arena so that they could be rushed by lions, tigers, bears, and other wild beasts.

The condemned were often tied up or otherwise rendered unable to defend themselves so that the animals could feast upon them with abandon. Such spectacles were often advertised for several days in advance, with special placards put in place along roads in and out of the city. These advertising campaigns made sure that the seats in the Colosseum were packed with visitors, from both near and far, who wished to feast their eyes upon the destruction of the condemned.

One of the most famous Christians who were condemned to be destroyed in the Colosseum was supposedly none other than the Apostle John. John, also known as John the Revelator due to his contributions to the Book of Revelation, was one of the original twelve disciples of Jesus Christ. John stands out as the only disciple who managed to die of natural causes and live a long life. In fact, John is said to have lived all the way until 100 CE (although some sources say 98 CE), passing at the ripe old age of ninety-four years old.

But according to Christian tradition, it was only with God's help that this apostle managed to do so. Other biblical sources on John allege that during the reign of Domitian (r. 81–96 CE), the Romans attempted to execute this long-lived apostle right in the middle of the Roman Colosseum before thousands of screaming spectators. In their gruesome excess, his executioners had concocted a scheme in which John would be dunked into a vat of boiling oil.

The oil was fired up to a super-hot temperature. John was hauled out, and a couple of Roman soldiers picked him up and threw him right in. But according to tradition, once submerged, John remained miraculously unscathed. He simply stood there in the midst of the boiling cauldron, none the worse for wear. It's said that the thousands of Roman spectators who bore witness to this event were so touched by it that they began converting to Christianity on the spot.

This was most certainly not what John's Roman persecutors had in mind! It was supposedly after this failed attempt on the Apostle John's life that his captors gave up the idea of killing him and instead simply exiled him to the Greek island of Patmos. And according to Christian tradition, it was on Patmos that John had his vision and wrote what would become the final chapter of the Christian Bible: the Book of Revelation.

There is no hard evidence that John was miraculously spared death in the Roman Colosseum. And as such, whether or not it actually happened is more or less a matter of faith. At any rate, one Christian martyr whose demise is clearly documented is one of the Apostle John's very own disciples—Saint Ignatius.

Ignatius was, at one point, chosen to be the bishop of Antioch in Asia Minor. Although the details are not clear, it appears that he, too, was caught up in Roman persecution, as he was arrested and hauled off to Rome to await his fate sometime during his tenure as bishop. It is said that Ignatius was taken into Roman custody during the reign of Domitian's successor, Emperor Trajan, who reigned from 98 to 117 CE.

According to tradition, during the journey to Rome, Ignatius was able to write many letters, which were sent to local churches along the way. These letters provide some historical documentation for what may have actually happened to Ignatius. Some are skeptical of the letters, however, insisting that it wouldn't make sense for the Romans to allow Ignatius the privilege of writing them. Furthermore, these detractors contend, the Romans would have taken Ignatius by boat directly to Rome rather than overland. If this were the case, he wouldn't have had the opportunity to drop off letters.

At any rate, around the year 108, he ended up being condemned to the Colosseum, where he wasn't exactly thrown to lions but was rather left standing in the middle of the Colosseum as lions were *thrown at him*. Traditional accounts tell us that Saint Ignatius was attacked by at least two lions, which promptly began feeding upon the martyr. It's said that Saint Ignatius did not panic and run from the beasts but stoically accepted his fate, offering no resistance as the lions tore him apart.

It was a fate, in fact, that Ignatius had apparently already anticipated. He even mentioned it in one of the letters he is said to have left for Roman Christians. The letter read, in part, "I am writing to all the churches and am insisting to everyone that I die for God of my own free will—unless you hinder me. I implore you: do not be unseasonably kind to me. Let me be food for the wild beasts, through whom I can reach God. I am God's wheat, and I am being ground by the teeth of the wild beasts, that I may be found pure bread of Christ."

If the letters attributed to Ignatius are indeed authentic, it would seem that Ignatius successfully foresaw the grisly fate that would await him when he was forced to participate in one of Rome's warped games. Decades after Ignatius was martyred, one of his previous associates, Polycarp, the Bishop of Smyrna, was martyred, dying around 150. Polycarp, an esteemed church father at the time of his demise, was widely admired for the bravery and courage that he showed in the arena.

In the Christian text, *The Martyrdom of Polycarp*, these feelings take center stage. In it, the Christian writer proclaims, "We are writing to you, dear brothers, the story of the martyrs and of blessed Polycarp who put a stop to the persecution by his own martyrdom as though he were putting a seal upon it...Just as the Lord did, he too waited that he might be delivered up, that we might become his imitators...Who indeed would not admire the martyrs' nobility, their courage, their love of the Master? For even when they were torn by whips until the very structure of their bodies was laid bare down to the inner veins and arteries, they endured it, making even the bystanders weep for pity."

After these words of encouragement and exultation, the writer then goes on to state, "As Polycarp entered the amphitheater, a voice from heaven said: 'Be strong, Polycarp, and have courage.' No one saw who was speaking, but those of our people who were present heard the voice. Then, as he was brought in, a great shout arose when the people heard that it was Polycarp who had been arrested. As he was brought before him, the governor asked him: 'Are you Polycarp?' And when he admitted he was the governor tried to persuade him to recant, saying: 'Have respect for your age'; [and other similar things that they are accustomed to say]; 'swear by the Genius of the emperor. Recant. Say, "Away with the atheists!"'"

The account then goes on to state, "Polycarp, with a sober countenance, looked at all the mob of lawless pagans who were in the arena, and shaking his fist at them, groaned, looked up to heaven, and said: 'Away with the atheists!' The governor persisted and said: 'Swear and I will let you go. Curse Christ!' But Polycarp answered: 'For eighty-six years I have been his servant and he has done me no wrong. How can I blaspheme against my kind and savior?'" Polycarp had been a Christian for decades, and even when threatened with force, he was unwilling to bend. His persecutors, infuriated at his refusal to recant, had Polycarp set on fire and burned alive in the arena.

Another famous Christian martyr to face death in the Roman games was a young woman by the name of Vibia Perpetua. Vibia Perpetua came under Roman scrutiny around 202 CE when she refused to pay homage to the Roman emperor. Quite contrary to the image of aged Christian saints, such as the Apostle John or even Saint Ignatius, facing off against Roman persecution, Perpetua was a newlywed young mother in her early twenties when she faced Rome's wrath.

As the story goes, this young Christian's life was interrupted when she and her local group of Christians came to the attention of Roman authorities in her hometown of Carthage. Upon being confronted by Roman officials, she refused to perform the obligatory sacrifice to the emperor. Even though her own father begged her to renounce her faith so she could live, Perpetua steadfastly refused.

Perpetua was from a rich and well-educated family. And the fact that she was secretly practicing Christianity was a deep embarrassment to them. However, the fact that Perpetua was an educated woman from the 3rd century proved to be a great gift for Christian literature due to the fact that she was an epic diary writer and documented many of her own thoughts and experiences.

She continued to write even after her arrest, at one point making the vivid entry, "Oh bitter day! There was a great heat because of the closeness of the air, there was cruel handling by the soldiers. Lastly I was tormented by concern for my baby." Yes, perhaps the worst part of Perpetua's confinement was the fact that she had been separated from her child. She documents how her father pleaded with her until the very end to simply renounce her faith.

If she had simply given up being a Christian (or simply pretended to do so) and then paid the traditional respects to the emperor, she would have been allowed to live and would have had all of her previous freedoms restored. She noted in her diary how her own father had so desperately sought to persuade her of such.

She recalled one such attempt, in which her dear old dad pleaded, "Have pity, daughter, on my grey hairs; have pity on your father, if I am worthy to be called father by you—don't give me over to the scorn of men. Think of your brothers; your mother, your aunt. Consider your son, who will not live long if you die. Give up your resolution; do not destroy us all."

Think what you will about her father's efforts to dissuade her, but this is quite obviously a man who loved his child and sought to bring her back from the brink of destruction. Yet, Perpetua was resolute in her decision, and she refused to back down. During her trial, her father continued to plead with her. At one point, he even held up her little son, urging her, "Perform the sacrifice! Have mercy on the child!"

This, of course, was done to remind her of how much of a hardship her son would have, to grow up without his mother, if she refused to recant and offer sacrifice to the emperor. Nevertheless, Perpetua continued to refuse, simply stating, "I am a Christian." In the end, the Roman procurator—a man named Hilarian—brought down the final verdict as it pertained to Perpetua's fate. She would be fed to the lions in the Roman Colosseum.

The night prior to her execution, Perpetua had a strange dream. She dreamed that she was in the arena, forced into gladiatorial combat against an "Egyptian opponent." Moments later, her clothing fell away, and she found that she had been transformed into a man. She then proceeds to wrestle the Egyptian to a standstill until she is declared the winner and led through the gates of the arena, victorious.

Despite what one might interpret from such a dream, Perpetua did not view it as an indication of a worldly victory in the ring but rather a spiritual victory over the devil. Perpetua interpreted her Egyptian opponent as being the devil in disguise (as Egypt was often Israel's enemy in the Old Testament) and that her passing through the gate was an indication of her arrival in heaven after being martyred.

Her dreams were indeed prophetic. She and her fellow condemned Christians were taken out into the arena on the day of their condemnation, and wild animals were set loose upon them. The beasts only managed to kill two among the group, however, so a gladiator was called in to dispatch the rest. This man was able to quickly kill all of the condemned, but when Perpetua's time came, it's said that, for some reason, he lost his nerve and accidentally botched her execution.

Instead of slitting her throat, he cleaved right into bone, causing terrible pain and suffering. Nevertheless, Perpetua gathered what remained of her dwindling strength and directed her killer's knife back to her throat, aiding him in the very act of cutting her down.

Even though Christians often met a grisly end in the Roman games, it would be Christians who would play a major role in eliminating them. For it was after the Roman Empire became predominantly Christian in its makeup that the blood sports of the past were eliminated entirely. Centuries of persecution made it clear that the Christian faithful could not be dissuaded from their beliefs by way of force. If anything, it only emboldened the Christians even more. The Roman government wanted to eliminate Christianity as an alternative belief system, yet Christians were becoming all the more militant in the face of persecution.

In the mid-3rd century, Cyprian, the Bishop of Carthage, captured this sense of urgent militancy well. During one of the great persecutions of the day, he wrote his so-called "Letter to the Martyrs" to address this very notion.

Cyprian declared, "The multitude of those who were present saw with admiration the heavenly contest, the contest of God the spiritual contest, the battle of Christ, saw that his servants stood with free voice, with unyielding mind, with divine virtue—bare indeed, of weapons of this world, but believing and armed with weapons of faith. The tortured stood more bravely than the torturers; and the limbs, beaten and torn as they were, overcame the hooks that beat and tore them."

He then elaborates, "The scourge, often used again and again with all its rage, could not conquer invincible faith, even though the membrane which enclosed the guts were broken, and it was no longer the limbs but the wounds of the servants of God that were being tortured. Blood was flowing which would quench the blaze of persecution, which would overcome the flames of Gehenna with its glorious gore. Oh, what a spectacle was that to the Lord, how sublime, how great, how acceptable to the eyes of God in the allegiance and devotion of his soldiers!"

The Christian leader then goes on to urge his fellow Christians, "If the battle shall call you out, if the day of your contest shall come, engage bravely, fight with constancy, knowing that you are fighting under the eyes of a present Lord, that you are attaining by the confession of his name to his own glory...He only looks on his servants, but he himself also wrestles in us, himself is engaged, himself also in the struggles of our conflict not only crowns, but is crowned."

Christian persecution in the Roman Empire would only end with the Edict of Milan in 313 CE. This edict, issued by Roman Emperor Constantine and his co-emperor Valerius Licinianus Licinius, stipulated that Christianity would be recognized as a legal religion and forbade any further persecution of the faith. The influence of Christianity would continue to grow in the meantime, and by 380, it would be made the official state religion of the Roman Empire under Roman Emperor Theodosius.

By this time, the old Roman games of the arena looked more and more like pagan relics of the past. For Christians, these vestiges of Rome's pagan roots would soon become an intolerable eyesore. Saint Augustine, a contemporary of the time, even went as far as to say that the practice of these old traditions was akin to conjuring up demons.

An excerpt from Saint Augustine's *Sermons* tells us, "For such demons are pleased with misleading songs, with worthless shows, with varied foulness of the theatre, with the frenzy of the games, with cruelty of the amphitheater, with the violent contests of those who undertake strife and controversy provocative even of hostility in their support of noxious characters, for instance, of an actor in a mime, a play, or a pantomime, of a charioteer, or of a venator. By acting in this way that, as it were, offer incense to the demons within their hearts. For the deceptive spirits rejoice in seduction they feast upon the evil customs and the notoriously vile life of those whom they have misled and entrapped."

The Roman games did indeed spring from religious practices, and Saint Augustine, now speaking as a leader of the newly Christianized Roman Empire, reinterpreted the games as nothing short of the worship of demonic influences. To Augustine, the spectacle of violence, lust, and all the other vices of the arena could only be seen as an offering of "incense" to the demonic forces that thrive on such negative energy. Whether demonic entities were literally hovering around the arena to lap up the negative emotions that were unleashed is anyone's guess, but Augustine's words certainly struck a chord with his audience.

And the newly Christianized Rome was most certainly finding the old Roman games to be a source of embarrassment and shame rather than something to celebrate or be proud of. Christian thinker Aurelius Prudentius Clemens, more commonly known as simply Prudentius, was even more explicit when he directly drew a connection between the deaths of gladiators in the colosseums with human sacrifices to pagan gods.

In the text *Books Against Symmachus*, Prudentius proclaimed, "Look at the crime-stained offerings to frightful Dis, to whom is sacrificed the gladiator laid low on the ill starred arena, a victim offered to Phlegethon in misconceived expiation for Rome. For what means that senseless show with its exhibition of sinful skill, the killing of young men, the pleasure fed on blood, the deathly dust that ever enshrouds the spectators, the grim sight of the parade in the amphitheater?"

Invoking the name of the Roman god of death, who was so often portrayed in the Roman games, Prudentius then rails, "Why, Charon by the murder of these poor wretches receives offerings that pay for his services as guide, and is propagated by a crime in the name of religion. Such are the delights of the Jupiter of the dead, such the acts in which the ruler of dark Avernus finds content and refreshment. Is it not shameful that a strong imperial nation thinks it needful to offer such sacrifices for its country's welfare and seeks the help of religion from the vaults of hell?"

As Christianity became more entrenched in Roman society, the Roman games were becoming increasingly out of step with many. As the old traditions became more and more marginalized, they were soon cast aside entirely, and as Prudentius would say, they were eventually consigned to the vaults of hell.

Chapter 6 – Extravagant Military Reenactments

"A noble man compares and estimates himself by an idea which is higher than himself; and a mean man, by one lower than himself. The one produces aspiration; the other ambition, which is the way in which a vulgar man aspires."

-Roman emperor, Marcus Aurelius

Along with gladiatorial fighting, wild beast hunts, and even throwing prisoners to the lions, the Roman games often boasted extravagant military reenactments. The arena could be flooded for naval reenactments, or flora and fauna from faraway lands could be inserted into the sands to imply a foreign battlefield. It was on these backdrops that grand military dramas for the masses were orchestrated.

Interestingly, the wild and untamed lands of Britain were a favorite backdrop at the Roman games. In particular, the rapid-fire fighting of Celtic tribes on horseback and chariot were emulated on a grand scale. Celtic warriors were even imported to participate in the battles. During the days of the Roman Republic, military triumphs such as these were standard fare.

Roman historian Livy leaves us an excellent record of what they were like. Livy recorded, "It was the custom in those days, before the introduction of the modern extravagance of filling the arena with wild beasts from all over the world, to seek out spectacular performances of all kinds; for one race with quadrigae [chariot drawn with four horses] and one bareback display scarcely took up an hour for the two events. In one of these displays, groups of about sixty young men [sometimes more in the more elaborate games] entered the arena under arms."

He then goes on to state, "Their act was to some extent an imitation of army maneuvers, but in other respects it demanded a more sophisticated skill than that of ordinary soldiers, and it had more in common with the style of gladiatorial combats After performing various evolutions they would form in order of battle, with shields massed together over their heads, the front rank standing, the second stooping a little, the third and fourth increasing their stoop, and the rear rank kneeling, the whole forming a 'tortoise' with a slope like the roof of a house."

What's being described is actually a classic Roman battle formation, in which shield formations in the front, with the shields raised tightly over the Romans' heads, created an impervious barrier. Romans would use this famed "tortoise" formation to essentially create a human tank that could march toward enemies even under a heavy onslaught of enemy arrows.

Livy then goes on to explain, "From this, two armed men would rush out, about fifty feet away from each other, and, after making threatening gestures at one another they would climb up from the bottom to the top of the 'tortoise' over the close packed shields. They would then perform a kind of skirmish along the outer edges of the 'tortoise,' or engage in combat in the center leaping about just as if on solid ground." This testimony bears perfect witness to the pomp and circumstance of military reenactments during the Roman games.

Emperor Claudius, who reigned from 41 to 54 CE, was an emperor particularly keen on celebrating Rome's military prowess by staging massive triumphal displays. During these events, which recreated Rome's triumph over Britain, Claudius ditched his traditional imperial garb for the dress of a grand general of the Roman armed forces in an effort to further solidify his image as the most powerful man in the Roman Empire.

However, it was the naval battles that seemed to have captured the Roman public's imagination like no other. Many of these mock naval battles, or as the Romans called them, *naumachiae*, were held at Fucine Lake (also known as Lake Fucino) in central Italy. In 52 CE, Emperor Claudius held a grand affair on the lake in which two whole fleets, consisting of some twenty-five ships each, waged war against each other.

Although these are referred to as "mock naval battles," the fighting was real since tens of thousands of condemned prisoners were forced to do battle with each other across the decks of these crafts or even on wooden bridges erected over the waters. To make sure that these naval gladiators put on a good show and didn't try to run off, the whole lake was ringed with Roman troops.

Some of the troops even actively manned catapults at the perimeter of the lake, more than ready to bombard a craft with stone boulders if the pilots of that craft were to go off script and attempt to race to the shore to escape. During Claudius's exercise in 52 CE, the condemned men apparently put on a very good show for the masses in attendance of the Roman games that day.

And the preparation for all of this was immense in scope. Roman historian Tacitus described it as thus, "Nearly at this date, the tunneling of the mountain between Lake Fucinus and the river Liris had been achieved; and, in order that the impressive character of the work might be viewed by a larger number of the visitants, a naval battle was arranged upon the lake itself."

Tacitus then goes on to say, "Claudius equipped triremes, quadriremes, and nineteen thousand combatants: the lists he surrounded with rafts, so as to leave no unauthorized points of escape, but reserved space enough in the center to display the vigor of the rowing, the arts of the helmsman, the impetus of the galleys, and the usual incidents of an engagement. On the rafts were stationed companies and squadrons of the praetorian cohorts, covered by a breastwork from which to operate their catapults and ballistae: the rest of the lake was occupied by marines with decked vessels."

Tacitus then concludes, "He and Agrippina presided, the one in a gorgeous military cloak, the other—not far distant—in a Greek mantle of cloth of gold. The battle, though one of criminals, was contested with the spirit and courage of freemen; and, after much blood had flowed, the combatants were exempted from destruction." Yes, Claudius was so pleased with the efforts that pardons were in order.

Claudius's successor, Nero, held even more extravagant mock military games. He was known to start off his games with an animal hunt before flooding the entire arena so that reenactments of great naval battles could be displayed. After this, he would then drain the arena and host gladiator matches on the dry ground before flooding it once again just so he could invite the spectators to a lavish banquet held on board a huge floating craft.

As mad and deranged as Emperor Nero has been characterized to be over the centuries, he certainly knew how to please Roman audiences when it came to the Roman games. But not everyone appreciated his efforts.

Later, the Roman historian Tacitus in his *Annals* criticized the emperor, writing, "Nero himself now tried to make it appear that Rome was his favorite abode. He gave feasts in public places as if the whole city were his own home. But the most prodigal and notorious banquet was given by Tigellinus. To avoid repetitious accounts of extravagance, I shall describe it, as a model of its kind."

Tacitus then further elaborated, "The entertainment took place on a raft constructed on Marcus Agrippa's lake. It was towed about by other vessels, with gold and ivory fittings. Their rowers were degenerates, assorted according to age and vice. Tigellinus had also collected birds and animals from remote countries, and even the products of the ocean. On the quays were brothels stocked with high ranking ladies. Opposite them could be seen naked prostitutes, indecently posturing and gesturing. At nightfall the woods and houses nearby echoed with singing and blazed with lights."

Emperor Titus later inaugurated the Roman games at the Roman Colosseum in 80 CE with some rather extravagant reenactments of his own. He began the show with the slaughter of animals in massive beast hunts, which was quite common at the time. But what really galvanized the masses was the military reenactments at the end. As the Roman writer and historian Cassius Dio recorded, "There was a battle between cranes and also between four elephants; animals both tame and wild were slain to the number of nine thousand; and women [not those of any prominence, however] took part in dispatching them. As for the men, several fought in single combat and several groups contended together both in infantry and naval battles."

Dio then continues, "For Titus suddenly filled the same theatre with water and brought in horses and bulls and some other domesticated animals that had been taught to behave in the liquid element just as on land. He also brought in people on ships, who engaged in a sea-fight there, impersonating the Corcyraeans and Corinthians; and others gave a similar exhibition outside the city in the grove of Gaius and Lucius, a place which Augustus had once excavated for this very purpose. There, too, on the first day there was a gladiatorial exhibition and wild-beast hunt, the lake in front of the images having first been covered over with a platform of planks and wooden stands erected around it. On the second day there was a horse-race, and on the third day a naval battle between three thousand men, followed by an infantry battle. The 'Athenians' conquered the

'Syracusans' [these were the names the combatants used], made a landing on the islet and assaulted and captured a wall that had been constructed around the monument. These were the spectacles that were offered, and they continued for a hundred days."

All of these grand displays of raw power that Cassius Dio describes were meant to demonstrate the greatness of Rome in general and Titus in particular. Probably the most infamous Roman "triumphal" display over an enemy came in the aftermath of the so-called "Jewish War" that destroyed the Jewish temple in Jerusalem and brought countless Jewish freedom fighters, who were now prisoners of war, directly to Rome and its Roman games. Roman Jewish historian Flavius Josephus recorded how these prisoners of war eventually became fodder for military-inspired Roman games under Titus.

Josephus relates, "During his stay at Caesarea Maritima, Titus celebrated his brother's birthday with great splendor, reserving for his honor much of the punishment of his Jewish captives. For the number of those destroyed in contests with wild beasts or with one another or in the flames was more than two thousand five hundred. Yet to the Romans, notwithstanding the myriad forms in which their victims perished, all this seemed too light a penalty. After this, [Titus] Caesar passed to Beirut, a city of Phoenicia and a Roman colony."

He then furthers stresses, "Here he [Titus] made a longer stay, displaying still greater magnificence on the occasion of his father's birthday, both in the costliness of the spectacles and in the ingenuity of the various other items of expenditure. Multitudes of captives perished in the same manner as before. Leaving from Beirut, Titus exhibited costly spectacles in all the cities of Syria he passed through, making his Jewish captives serve to display their own destruction."

It's interesting to note that along with the famous Colosseum in Rome, the Romans were in the habit of building temporary amphitheaters in far-flung corners all over the Roman Empire. These amphitheaters were often built on the frontiers, and for the Romans, they had militaristic as well as entertainment value. These constructions were often built by the soldiers themselves and doubled as training grounds for the troops stationed in those frontier regions.

The structures proved to be great propaganda platforms for the Romans as it pertained to demonstrating Roman power to subjected peoples. Newly conquered groups would even be invited to attend martial demonstrations of Roman military might. These served not only as a means to entertain and pacify the locals but also to clearly demonstrate to them the power of their overlords.

The structures were also important as a backup fortification should the local populace of the frontier regions get restless and turn aggressive against the Roman occupiers. Such military-styled amphitheaters can be found in Britain, France, and many other frontier regions held by the former Roman Empire.

Chapter 7 – Commodus: The Emperor Turned Gladiator

"While all Greece honored an Olympic victor and to go onstage as a spectacle for the people was held in no way shameful to them, all these things are considered by us to be infamia, humilia—and far from honorable."

-Roman biographer, Cornelius Nepos

Roman Emperor Lucius Aurelius Commodus came into this world on August 31ˢᵗ, 161. Upon becoming emperor in 176, Commodus is said to have boasted that he was "born both man and emperor." This was in reference to the fact that he was the son of Marcus Aurelius, with whom he co-reigned from 176 to 180, the year Aurelius perished. Afterward, Commodus would continue to rule Rome on his own, with his reign only coming to an end in the year 192.

Interestingly enough, however, his political enemies long whispered that Commodus wasn't the son of an emperor at all but rather was the product of an illicit union between his mother, Faustina, and a gladiator. The gladiators (at least those who truly tried to compete in the ring) were the heartthrobs and bad boys of Rome, and some of them really did have affairs with noble Roman women.

But it has not been determined if Commodus's mother was one of them. Nevertheless, it is rather astonishing how fascinated Emperor Commodus would become with the Roman games and gladiatorial combat. In fact, he would insist on throwing himself personally into the ring. It seems that Commodus's first taste of Roman spectacle occurred as a child when his father's co-emperor (and Commodus's namesake), Lucius Aurelius Verus, held a military triumph to commemorate Rome's recent victories over the empire's eastern enemies, the Parthians.

This triumphal event imbued much of the past pageantry of the Roman games, with sacred white bulls being marched by the spectators as they were led to their ultimate destination—to become a sacrifice to the Roman deity Jupiter. These were followed by the spoils of war, the various goods and treasures pilfered from the enemy, which were paraded before all. Next, actual prisoners of war were showcased, all of them marching off toward the games held in the Roman Colosseum.

Co-emperors Marcus Aurelius and Lucius Aurelius Verus were both in attendance, and more than likely, so was little Commodus. And if so, it was likely this event that heralded his first exposure to the excitement of the Roman games. His father, Marcus Aurelius, was not a fan of the games, especially detesting the blood sports that often took place. In one incredible instance, it is said that Marcus was so disturbed by the pain inflicted on an acrobatic performer who accidentally fell to the ground that he had specially cushioned matting placed on the floor of the arena to soften any such future falls. He is also said to have occasionally ordered the gladiators to fight with blunted weapons to prevent the spilling of blood.

Marcus Aurelius, a man known for his stoic philosophy and moderation, did not wish to see violence in the ring. Commodus, on the other hand, would grow incredibly fond of the Roman games and all of its bloody trappings. It wasn't long before he himself began to train his body in anticipation of participating in the games himself.

In fact, history tells us that it was while Commodus was training at a "wrestling school" as a young man that he faced his first brush with death. It wasn't due to the strong arms of a fellow wrestler that Commodus nearly perished but rather the sudden onset of illness. He was said to have been "seized by a hot fever." Fortunately, for Commodus, he had one of the best doctors at his disposal—the Roman physician Galen.

As young Commodus's health seemed to rapidly deteriorate, Galen quickly took charge of the situation, having the future emperor "gargle" a concoction of "honey and rose water." The treatment seemed to do the trick, and to the amazement of everyone, Commodus's health was restored. And in that fateful year of 176, when Commodus first became co-emperor with his father Marcus Aurelius, he got to see firsthand how important the Roman games were to the people and to Roman political governance itself.

For it was that fall that he joined his father for an appearance at the games in Rome, in which his father gave a public speech about Rome's political state. Not only did Aurelius speak, but the crowd also answered back, requesting gratuities from the emperor. Even though the Roman Empire was cash-strapped at the time, Marcus Aurelius obliged, generously handing out gold coins to the crowd.

Commodus learned a valuable lesson that day as to both the power of the Roman games and the power the spectators had over the emperor. Shortly thereafter, on December 23rd, 176, a special "triumphal chariot race" was held, in which Commodus played a part. Here, Commodus paraded around the track in grand display. He also handed out gold coinage and other prizes to the spectators. Just a few years later, in 180, Commodus's father and co-emperor, Marcus Aurelius, passed, making Commodus the sole ruler of the realm.

Commodus had a lot on his plate, but he still had time to indulge in gladiatorial contests. In addition to that, he also began heavily training for them himself. Fascinated with the Roman games, Commodus took on the trappings of a gladiator known as the Secutor.

These gladiators were heavily armed with solid helmets that granted limited vision. They also came equipped with an oblong shield, otherwise known as a *scutum*, as well as a short sword known as a *gladius*.

This type of gladiator was often paired with the Retiarius, who wielded a net and a trident and usually attempted to poke, prod, and parry their opponents, all while attempting to ensnare them in their net. Before ever going into the arena himself, Commodus quietly trained in private, competing with a gladiator in private sessions outside of the Colosseum.

These were friendly matches in which carefully selected associates would practice with him. Rather than duels to the death, the rounds would typically end with his opponent indicating defeat by removing their shield and lifting their index finger into the air. This would signal that Commodus had won the match, and he would stop engaging his opponent. Not everything always worked out as planned, however, and it is said that Commodus actually killed one of his training partners by accident on at least one occasion. He also apparently injured a few others. Some accounts report that he accidentally chopped off a nose in one instance and an ear in another.

Along with these instances of one-on-one combat, Commodus also practiced hunting animals on his own personal training grounds. The activity that probably took up the most of his time, however, was his practice runs on the track, racing chariots.

For this, he spared no expense, buying himself the best equipment, uniform, and horses for the enterprise. In addition to using his own private estate as his training grounds, Commodus is said to have even practiced at the official gladiator training school, located just outside of the Colosseum. Soon enough, however, Commodus himself would be performing in the arena as a gladiator. This horrified much of the Roman elite since it was considered scandalous for a noble Roman— let alone an emperor—to participate in the Roman games.

Nevertheless, Commodus took center stage in the Colosseum on wild beast hunts and in gladiatorial matches. It was the latter of which that would be the most shocking since Commodus had a penchant of wanting to be paired with disabled veterans or disadvantaged Roman citizens who were missing a leg so they couldn't walk. He also sought out those missing an arm or two, as they couldn't properly defend themselves. He would easily run through these poor, hapless souls with his sword.

Considering how much Commodus sought to be a heroic figure (he often likened himself to a reincarnated Hercules), it's appalling how cowardly his exploits in the arena truly were. Rome's economy began to suffer in the meantime due to the extravagance that Commodus routinely made use of during his cameos at the Roman games. Things became so bad, in fact, that the Roman currency became devalued.

Finally, in 190, Commodus, having grown weary of having to govern his empire (it took too much time away from training to be a gladiator), decided to hand over all daily governance to his top advisor, a former slave by the name of Cleander. Shortly after Cleander took over, the Roman Empire was rocked by famine.

Commodus was then conveniently able to blame the whole fiasco on Cleander, insisting that he was in charge of such matters. As the rancor against Cleander built among the populace, Commodus attended a series of Roman games during which he readily listened while an angry public clamored against Cleander.

The games were indeed an allowed space for the public to lodge their grievances to the emperor. It has been theorized, however, that much of this displeasure was organized behind the scenes in a highly orchestrated attempt to malign Cleander since he would have been officiating the games. The Roman historian Herodian seemed to capture this sentiment at work. He noted at the time how the public had "organized themselves in the theatres and shouted insults at him [Cleander] all together."

At any rate, the theatrics worked, and Commodus stepped up to answer the public's outcry against his top manager of affairs. Shortly after, he had Cleander summarily executed and his head placed on the tip of a spear for all to see in order to satiate the displeasure of the Roman public.

It has been said that Rome's people cried out for "bread and circuses" during this period. The wily Commodus, realizing a grain shortage would lead to a bread shortage, must have been hoping that the populace would be happy with at least one circus if they couldn't have the other. And in the year 192, in pursuit of providing the latter, Commodus hosted his famous Plebeian Games.

Here, Commodus not only hosted extravagant Roman games for the masses but also took center stage. Every morning at the start of the games, he would galivant around for a grand animal hunt in which he killed countless wild beasts by way of his spear and bow and arrows. There was more to come, however. By late December, it had been announced that the emperor himself would kick off the year 193 by hosting Roman games in which he would personally perform as a gladiator.

He would not live to see the day, though, since the immediate backlash that such talk sparked led to renewed conspiratorial intrigue against Commodus. All this conspiratorial talk would lead to Commodus's death on December 31st, 192. First, his mistress tried to poison him, but when this attempt failed, a trained wrestler was called in to finish Commodus off. It must have seemed ironically fitting that his life was ended in a form of martial combat straight out of the Roman games that Commodus so loved.

Chapter 8 – Chariot Races: The Roman Indy 500

"For at first there were only two colors: white and red. White was sacred to Winter because of the whiteness of its snow; red, to Summer because of the redness of the sun. But afterwards, when both love of pleasure and superstition had grown apace, some dedicated the red to Mars, others the white to the Zephyrs, the green to Mother Earth or Spring, the blue to Sky and Sea or Autumn.

-Christian writer, Tertullian

In the United States, the start of summer isn't complete without a running of the famous Indianapolis 500. For those who aren't aware of this American tradition, it consists of a four-hour-long race around a circular track by Formula One race cars hurling about at terrific speeds. Fans flock to Indianapolis, Indiana, from all over to see the so-called "Greatest Spectacle in Racing."

Along with the thrill of the speed, some (even though they might not admit it) are no doubt excited to see some of the inevitable car crashes as well. And it was very much the same in the days of Rome when folks would gather around a track to see not cars but horse-drawn chariots rushing around a race track. Romans would pick the chariot drivers they wished to win and root for their heroes. They would also stand and gape at the many dangerous and deadly wrecks that occurred.

But unlike the Indy 500, the Roman chariot racers didn't just crash on accident; sometimes, they would intentionally force each other off the road. It was quite common for these violent chariot races to end in both fatalities and severe injuries. Chariot racers employed fast yet flimsy chariots that were not at all well protected. The strategy was to be fast and not get hit by your opponent, but one wrong turn or a swipe from an adversary could easily lead to a charioteer's doom.

Interestingly enough, chariot races were one of the first to employ specific teams. These teams were designated by four specific colors, such as blue, green, red, and white. Fans would root for their team from the stands, and they would do so quite vigorously. On some occasions, fans would even spar with each other, and riots would erupt between fans of one team and another. During one chariot race, these riotous fans were so darned obnoxious that a Roman emperor in attendance—Emperor Vitellius—actually had them killed on the spot simply because they kept heckling the team he liked.

The race itself consisted of some seven laps around the track. There were seven egg-shaped, wooden objects placed around the track, and every time a lap was finished, one would be taken down to mark its completion. The races lasted for about fifteen minutes in total, and as many as twenty-four races could take place in one sitting. The location of chariot races was typically in a circus, and the famous Circus Maximus was a fan favorite. The term "Circus Maximus" basically translates as "biggest circus." This was the prime venue for racing chariots around a huge, circular track.

For the Romans, chariot racing was often the main event of their games. And according to writer and historian Roland Auguet, the Roman people actually believed that their very first chariot race dated all the way back to Rome's mythic founder, Romulus.

For those who are not aware of the legends behind Rome's founding, it is said that Romulus and his twin brother Remus were children of a woman named Rhea Silvia and the god of Mars. There's a lot to unpack in this Roman myth, but for the sake of simplicity, let's just say that somewhere in the twisting tides of fate, Romulus and Remus ended up being abandoned and raised by a "she-wolf." Yes, according to Roman legend, the mythic founders of Rome were literally thrown to the wolves. So, the story goes, it was actually the miraculous intervention of this she-wolf that saved these abandoned demigods' lives.

A conflict later erupted between Romulus, and he killed his brother. According to legend, a whole lot of drama ensued, but eventually, it's said that Romulus founded Rome. And when he did so, he was sure to host a few Roman games along the way. Writer and Roman researcher Roland Auguet is of the opinion that the original races were not chariot races as much as they were simple contests on horseback or even muleback.

By the time of Emperor Nero, however, an elaborate track for chariot races at the Circus Maximus was well established. It was established, but perhaps vulnerable would be a better description. The structures around the track were largely made of wood, and these would go up in flames during the Great Fire of Rome, which occurred in 64 CE, during Emperor Nero's reign.

As mentioned earlier in this book, it still remains somewhat unclear as to what may have caused this fire. Nero infamously blamed the Christians, but there is no evidence of any Christian saboteur. Others, in the meantime, would soon turn on Nero himself, theorizing that the ruler had purposely set fires as a form of ad-hoc demolition in order to remodel the Circus Maximus. The razed structures did indeed allow Nero to greatly modify and enhance the track when he built upon the ashes.

But there's no more evidence of Nero being an arsonist than there is that the Christians were. Nevertheless, Nero, who would commit suicide just a few years later, would go down in history as the one who "fiddled while Rome burned." Nero, despite his faults, was indeed a champion of the Roman games, chariot races in particular.

Nero, as mentioned, expanded the track at the Circus Maximus, and he also increased the number of games at the track, going from the standard twelve to a full twenty-four. Each of these matches was initiated by a game of chance or the so-called "drawing of lots." A charioteer standing in for each of the four teams (red, blue, green, and white) would cast lots to determine the starting positions. Once in place, these chariot racers would wait for their cue to take off, which was typically a piece of white fabric being thrown onto the track.

The chariots would then take off in a furious storm of pounding hoofbeats and grinding chariot wheels. These sounds were accompanied by the screaming spectators shouting out encouragement to their team of choice. The Roman Christian chronicler Tertullian described the experience, saying, "The praetor is too slow for [the fans]; all the time their eyes are rolling as though in rhythm with the lots he shakes up in his urn. Then they await the signal with bated breath; one outcry voices the common madness. Recognize the madness from their foolish behavior. 'He has thrown it!' they shout; everyone tells everybody else what all of them seen just that moment."

Tertullian seems to be annoyed at fans shouting their play-by-plays after the fact. But it's not any different than football fans at the Superbowl today, screaming that a team has made a touchdown when all the fans, as well as every TV in America, had already borne witness to it. Fans state the obvious not so much to inform but rather to punctuate the moment. Ancient spectators of the chariot races with their outbursts were no doubt doing much the same thing.

But spectators of the Roman games would take things to a whole other level through a little something called "curse tablets." Fans would literally try to invoke curses on the charioteers of the rival team. Writer and historian Alison Futrell has made note of one of these curse tablets found at a race track. The words of the curse tablet invoke an underworld deity and are glaringly blunt in purpose.

The tablet reads, "Most holy Lord Charakteres, tie up, bind the feet, the hands, the nerves, the eyes, the knees, the courage, the leaps, the whip, the victory and the crowning of Porphyras and Hapsicrates, who are in the middle-left, as well as his co-drivers of the Blue-colors in the stable of Eugenius. At the moment when they are about to compete may they not squeeze over, may they not collide, may they not extend, may they not force [us] out, may they not overtake, may they not break off [in a new direction] for the entire day when they are about to race. May they be broken, may they be draffed, may they be destroyed."

"May they be destroyed?" Really? Fans putting curses on rival players is more than a bit fanatical, to say the least. But that's just how seriously Romans took their games. It's interesting to note that in the later Roman Empire, after Christianity became the official religion of the state, such things were forbidden. But even so, fans would continue to try and hex their rivals in secret.

This was indicated in 364 CE when the son of Hilarinus, a charioteer, was accused of casting spells against his father's opponents. Alison Futrell quotes one Ammianus Marcellinus, who charged that Hilarinus had his son "instructed in certain secret practices forbidden by law, in order to use his help at home without other witnesses he was condemned to death."

The most dramatic part of the race was always the final lap. Here, the chariot racers were often neck and neck, and when one was desperately trying to edge out another, they would often attempt to literally run their opponents off the road. This was the moment in which these Roman games turned ugly, with chariot racers trying to grind their chariot wheels into the wheels of their opponents, all in an effort to break the wheel's axle, sending their adversary crashing to the side.

These crashes not only knocked the chariot racer out of the race, but on occasion, they also turned lethal. There are indeed many instances of charioteers falling from an out-of-control chariot and getting trampled by horses. Crashed chariots were called *naufragia*, which literally translates as "shipwrecks." Fans loved this drama and sat in rapt attention.

According to writer and researcher Roland Auguet, along with enjoying the show on the track, these spectators also enjoyed each other. The comradery was great among fans, especially among male and female fans. The audiences at the race track, you see, were not segregated by sex as the Colosseum would later be. And the track actually became known as a great place for lovers to hook up. According to some accounts, many of these spectators even consummated their love in the stands.

Roman poet Ovid humorously captures this experience at the Roman games in his whimsical piece called *The Art of Love*. Here, Ovid humorously instructs his readers, "Furthermore, don't overlook the meetings when horses are running; in the crowds at the track opportunity waits. There is no need for a code of finger-signals or nodding. Sit as close as you like; no one will stop you at all. In fact, you will have to sit close—that's one of the rules, at a race track. Whether she likes it or not, contact is part of the game."

After these remarks, Ovid then advises his readers, "Try to find something in common, to open the conversation; don't care too much what you say, just so that everyone hears. Ask her, 'Whose colors are those?'—that's good for an opening gambit. Put your own bet down fast, on whatever she plays. Then, when the gods come along in procession, ivory golden, outcheer every young man, shouting for Venus, the queen. Often it happens that dust may fall on the cloak of the lady. If such dust should fall, carefully brush it away. Even if there's no dust, brush off whatever there isn't. Any excuse will do: why do you think you have hands? If her cloak hangs low, and the ground is getting it dirty, gather it up with care, lift it a little, so! Maybe by the way of reward, and not without her indulgence, you'll be able to see ankle or possible knee. Then look around and glare at the fellow who's sitting behind you, don't let him crowd his knees into her delicate spine. Girls, as everyone knows, adore these little attentions: getting the cushion just right, that's in itself quite an art; yes, and it takes a technique in making a fan of your program or in fixing a stool under the feet of a girl."

Yes, more than a few Roman men were no doubt eager to see a little "ankle or possible knee" from female Roman fans. Ovid is obviously being humorous here, but such things certainly weren't without precedent. And romance at the games had worked quite well for none other than the Roman dictator Sulla during the days of the Roman Republic, for it was under similar circumstances in the stands of the Roman games that he met his future wife.

As the Roman historian Plutarch tells us, "There happened to be sitting near Sulla a very beautiful woman of a most distinguished family. Her name was Valeria. As she passed behind Sulla, she rested her hand on him, pulled off a little piece of wool from his toga and then went on to her seat. When Sulla looked round at her in surprise, she said, 'There's no reason to be surprised, Dictator. I only want to have a little bit of your good luck for myself.'"

Plutarch then goes on to say, "Sulla was far from displeased. After this they kept glancing at each other constantly turning their heads to look, and exchanging smiles. And in the end negotiations began for marriage." It seems that Sulla and his admirer were caught on the Roman equivalent of the "kiss cam" on the jumbotron. Everyone within radius now knew that Sulla and his admirer were quite smitten.

Besides the spectacle of racing and the spectacle of love-making, there were also additional acts on display, such as acrobatic circus-styled horse riding. It was a must-see event. And at this Roman version of the Indy 500, Romans were pleased with the spectacle on the track just as much as they were with the spectacle of each other.

Chapter 9 – The Gladiatrix: Female Gladiators in the Arena

"Illustrious Fame used to sing of the lion laid low in Nemea's spacious vale, Hercules' work. Let ancient testimony be silent, for after your shows, Caesar, we have now seen such things done by women's valor."

-Roman poet, Marcus Valerius Martialis

Although Rome, like much of the rest of the world at the time, was definitely a patriarchal society, strangely enough, there was some level of equality in the arena, as women were also allowed to fight. Female gladiators were always a good draw for spectators. Roman Emperor Nero, who reigned in the latter half of the 1ˢᵗ century CE, was among those who enjoyed the exploits of women warriors. Nero loved all things theatrical, and the extra flourish of female fighters appealed to his flair for the dramatic.

But not all Romans approved. Since gladiators were considered a lower class, it was considered dishonorable for women to participate. Laws were even enacted in an attempt to dissuade some of these more daring women from doing so. In fact, in 11 CE, the Roman Senate issued a *Senatus Consultum* or "Decree of the Senate," which stipulated age restrictions on women participating in the Roman games. These efforts were apparently made to keep youthful girls from being lured into the games.

One of the harshest critics of female participation in the Roman games was Roman historian Suetonius, who felt it dishonorable both to watch and for women to participate. Yet, the participation and spectating of these gladiatrices (feminine plural of gladiatrix) were fairly widespread. Roman Emperor Domitian, for one, seemed to enjoy female participation in the Roman games a great deal. Domitian, in fact, was known to host gladiatorial battles in which female warriors fought what in those days were termed "dwarves."

Yes, there wasn't much room for political correctness or even just plain correctness in the days of the Roman colosseums. The Roman citizens enjoyed such sideshows as well, and the arena was always packed for these events. It wasn't until the rule of Roman Emperor Septimius Severus in the third century CE that female participation in the Roman games was scaled back. Septimius Severus did not think it fitting for women to fight and eventually banned the practice outright.

There are plenty of records to indicate that female gladiators were a known quantity prior to the imperial ban. Emperor Domitian was the first emperor to preside over the fully-functioning Roman Colosseum, and the Roman poet Statius noted that Domitian sanctioned the participation of female fighters, who were associated with the legendary Amazons of Greek mythology.

Another Roman poet by the name of Marcus Valerius Martialis (better known simply as Martial) also alluded to Domitian's penchant for equality of the sexes in the arena when he wrote, "It is not enough that warrior Mars serves you in unconquered arms, Caesar. Venus herself serves you too."

Roman writer Juvenal held a pretty dismal view of all this as well. And in one of his epic written remarks on the subject, he stated, "What modesty can you expect in a woman who wears a helmet, abjures her own sex, and delights in feats of strength? Yet she would not choose to be a man, knowing the superior joys of womanhood. What a fine thing for a husband, at an auction of his wife's effects, to see her belt and armlets and plumes put up for sale, with a gaiter that covers half the left leg; or if she fights another sort of battle, how charmed you will be to see your young wife disposing of her greaves!"

Juvenal then goes on to declare, "Yet these are the women who find the thinnest of thin robes too hot for them; whose delicate flesh is chafed by the finest of silk tissue. See how she pants as she goes through her prescribed exercises; how she bends under the weight of her helmet; how big and coarse are the bandages which enclose her haunches; and then laugh when she lays down her arms and shows herself to be a woman!"

Juvenal and other Romans obviously held the practice of female gladiators in contempt and ridiculed the very notion of women participating in the Roman games. But, nevertheless, women were also fans of the Roman games, and in some circumstances, they did indeed actively participate. It seems the Romans were largely inspired by Greek tales of female warriors, and even the Greek pantheon of gods that made their way to Rome was most likely an inspiration for strong, robust, fighting women.

Pre-Christian Romans, after all, were known to have widely venerated the Greek goddesses of Athena and Minerva, who are both depicted as warriors who wielded weapons and engaged in battle. The Romans also looked toward recently conquered Britain, where female fighters were a very real part of the conflict. The Celtic Queen Boudica infamously led the Celts against the Romans around the year 60 CE. Although Boudica was ultimately defeated, being killed in the conflict, the conflict left scores of Roman soldiers, as well as civilians, in a bloody heap, buried in the rubble of what were once mighty Roman settlements, such as London.

London would be rebuilt, however, and in the restored city, new arenas would be forged in which Roman games would be played for the Roman settlers. And in these arenas, it wasn't long before a few women emerged to represent the mighty Celtic women who had fallen during Boudica's rebellion. The Romans were apparently both frightened and fascinated by the spectacle of these fierce female fighters.

Women who were either forced into the life of a gladiator or even those who chose it of their own volition would have been part of what was termed the *familia gladiatorum*. This was a special troupe of gladiators, which was controlled by a head honcho who managed the gladiatorial games in which this particular group of gladiators took part. Some troupe managers were harsh and brutal, but others could be somewhat kind and even protective of the gladiators who participated in the games under their watch. There are stories of these managers being particularly protective of female fighters under their care. But this, of course, was more likely the exception than the rule.

Much of the time, the handlers of the gladiatrix were about as callous and uncaring as they could be for those under their charge. This was demonstrated in 66 CE when, during the reign of Emperor Nero, Ethiopian female gladiators, as well as their own children, were made to do battle during a Roman game staged for the pleasure of the visiting Armenian Potentate, King Tridates I.

These Ethiopian gladiatrices apparently engaged in wild beast hunts, as well as combat with each other. It seems that while many Roman men did not take the idea of female fighters seriously, there were more than enough who were entertained by the sheer novelty of having women compete in the Roman games. And in many cases, the exotic nature of female combatants was reduced to an entirely absurd sideshow.

Under Domitian, for example, the gladiatrices often fought what the Romans called "dwarfs." Just imagine tall, muscular women locked in mortal combat with knife-wielding men of hereditarily short stature. Roman poet Publius Papinius Statius (better known as Statius) captures the absurdity of the moment. Statius chronicled the event, writing, "Women untrained to the rudis [a wooden sword given as an award to the victor] take their stand, daring, how recklessly, virile battles! You would think Termodon's bands were furiously fighting by Tanais or barbarous Phasis. Then comes a bold array of dwarves, whose term of growth abruptly ended has bound them once and for all into a knotted lump. They give and suffer wounds and threaten death—with fists how tiny! Father Mars and Bloody Virtus laugh, and cranes, waiting to swoop on scattered booty, marvel at the fiercer pugilists."

It's a little unclear what exactly Statius means by "knotted lump," but the contempt he has for the whole affair is pretty clear. But one of the most famous accounts of gladiatorial women in combat occurred in the 2nd century when it is said that two women referred to as "Achillia" and "Amazon" participated in the Roman games. The combatants seem to be what is known as *provactrices.*

Rather than being in one of the set categories of gladiators with specific gear that contrasted with their opponents' category, such as a Thraex and a Retiarii, the provactrices were participants who wore identical weapons and armor. Both female fighters are depicted with the same "leather-bound manicae" on their arms and the same type of "pleated and belted loincloths." They also had the same type of offensive weapons, with each participant wielding a "short sword." Their helmets, in the meantime, were cast to the side, displaying their similar tightly plaited hair wrapped around their heads. The climactic battle between these two is said to have ended in a draw, in which both women's lives were spared.

This strange age of female fighters would come to an end when Roman Emperor Septimius Severus banned the practice altogether in 200 CE.

Chapter 10 – Rome's Animal-Based Games

"Who does not reckon among the things of greatest interest the contests of gladiators and wild beasts, especially those which are given to you? But we, deeming that to see a man put to death is much the same as killing him, have abjured such spectacles."

-Christian writer, Athenagoras

This book has already covered, to some degree, the notion of wild animals being made part of the Roman games. The Romans used wild beasts to kill captives and even had gladiators battle them. Even Roman Emperor Commodus famously engaged wild beasts in the arena. But now, let's take a closer look at these animal-oriented games as a whole. Initially, the Romans held their main hunting games early in the day. This was the time the more respectable Romans were busy attending to their vocation. Thus, the fans present were most likely those without work or fresh-faced visitors to the city of Rome.

In many ways, the morning animal hunts were a warm-up for the later events that would be attended by the majority of the citizens later in the evening. Nevertheless, Roman authorities always made sure that the hunting games were elaborate and entertaining all the same.

According to writer and historian Roland Auguet, the hunting games themselves took on a greater life of their own as the Roman Empire progressed. Soon the games were being held later in the afternoon with a larger crowd of Romans in attendance.

Auguet also cites archaeological inscriptions that have been uncovered that seem to suggest that some of these animal hunts not only lasted until the afternoon but actually went on for several days at a time. The animal hunting games seemed to really come into their own by the time of the Roman Colosseum, as the high ramparts of the building provided a protective structure for spectators.

Before the Colosseum, the animals were much less secure. Temporary structures were created, and in some cases, deep ditches were dug to create a barrier between fans and animals, but the risk of something going wrong was much greater. The Colosseum, on the other hand, finally provided an entirely safe atmosphere in which spectators could watch wild beasts running around the arena without any fear of them being able to charge the stands.

Later, even further measures were taken to provide security, such as huge nets being put in place to prevent even the slightest possibility of a lion leaping or climbing over barriers and attacking fans. Before the Colosseum, animals were showcased in outside circuses such as Nero's Circus Maximus. For many of these events of the early Roman Empire, the main draw was simply seeing wild exotic animals from foreign lands, as they were not native to Rome. In true circus form, some of these animals were event taught to do a trick or two by their trainers.

Going even further back, to the last days of the Roman Republic, Roman General Pompey held lavish animal-based games in 79 BCE in which elephants, recently imported from Africa, were put on display to the delight of Roman citizens. However, Pompey did more than just show his elephants off; he also had skilled hunters bring the beasts down. Men skilled in hurling javelins threw their weapons right into the elephants' heads when they were in mid-charge. This stopped many of the elephants in their tracks, but for others, the spears missed, and they kept running. These then had spears hurled at their feet, thereby immobilizing them. Still, a few hobbled around on their knees before finally giving up and huddling in the center of the arena, reduced to nothing more than a pathetic wreck. As the dying elephants wailed to the heavens, many Romans were stricken with guilt at the sight and pitied the poor animals. It was a rare showing of remorse, an emotional feeling that was usually not felt while watching the Roman games.

Roman historian Dio Cassius captured this rare moment, recalling, "The elephants had withdrawn from the combat covered with wounds and walked about with their trunks raised towards heaven, lamenting so bitterly as to give rise to the report that they did not do so by mere chance but were crying out against the oaths in which they had trusted when they crossed over from Libya and calling upon heaven to avenge them! It was recalled that they had refused to board the ships before they received a pledge under oath from their drivers that no harm should come to them."

It remains unclear where the Romans got the notion that the elephants were "given oaths" by their handlers that if they left their native Libya for Rome that they would be well cared for. But the superstitious spectators seemed to believe that the wailing of the dying and betrayed beasts was more than merely their last gasp of life but rather an omen of Rome's coming doom. It is true that the Roman Republic would soon be on the verge of collapse, giving way to the Roman Empire, but to say that Rome's problems were due to the vengeance of a group of mistreated circus elephants is a bit of a stretch.

Despite Pompey's brutal takedown of the elephants, simply seeing a lion, tiger, or elephant, especially during the initial Roman games, was a real novelty. The novelty soon wore off, though, and seeing these wild beasts was not enough. It was then that the animals were actively hunted, made to attack prisoners, or even made to attack each other. It was quite common for a half-starved lion and half-starved bear to be poked and prodded into the arena and sent crashing into each other.

The thrill of seeing these two super predators, both from different far-flung parts of the Roman Empire, doing battle was usually a crowd favorite. In the first variation, the animal hunt had adequately armed men pursuing and hunting down animals. This game had its dangers, and even though they were well provisioned, it wouldn't be uncommon for a hunter to be killed or maimed for life. These hunters were at least armed and stood a chance.

However, the condemned prisoners that were thrown to the lions most certainly did not. Condemned prisoners were executed by the beasts by either being thrown without arms into the arena to be mauled to death or even by being tied up so that there was zero chance of them putting up any kind of resistance. The aforementioned beast matches, where wild animals fight one another, were truly a spectacle.

According to writer Roland Auguet, the most impressive of these specimens was the rhino. Auguet relates how, despite the rhino's power, it was a challenging animal to provoke. Roman handlers in the ring had to poke and prod the beast to get it to charge, and much of the time, it would rather just stand back and stare off into space than actually engage its adversaries. But once it did, the charge of the rhino was something to behold.

Auguet tells us that "neither the bulls it eviscerated like straw dummies nor the bears it threw into the air like puppies" could stand up to the wild charge of a fully engaged rhino. The most frequent pairing, however, was that of a lion facing off against a bull. The bull was important in Greek and Roman mythology, and to see this epic creature so easily dispatched by a lion was stunning to Roman audiences.

Some other more unusual pairings have also been documented. For example, there were instances when crocodiles were pitted against lions, a match that must have been rather intense. Some depictions recovered also suggest seals were sicced on bears, which seems a little unusual, to say the least. If animals were not being pitted together, one other variant of beast matches was having predatory animals, such as lions or even a pack of wild dogs, being sicced upon a group of prey animals, such as deer. Such things clearly show the decadent indulgence of the Romans. These slaughtered deer could have fed an army, but after allowing wild lions or dogs to mow them down, the animals perished simply for the blood lust of watching spectators.

The beasts procured by the Romans did not always cooperate with their handlers, however, and on some occasions, they could not even be brought into the ring. During the reign of Nero, one such game was memorable because of this very fact. A group of obstinate lions absolutely refused to be forced into the arena and put up such a resistance that they had to be slaughtered on the spot. It's unclear what substitute act was given for the waiting fans, but the promised games involving lions obviously were not available that day.

Along with violence perpetrated against animals, there were occasions in which more lighthearted and even comedic acts were introduced. Rome's animal circuses, in fact, had their own acrobatic routines in which animal trainers cavorted around and displayed feats of great gymnastic skill before hungry beasts. There are accounts of animal trainers being protectively encased in baskets and buffeted about by bewildered bears, which were completely unable to render harm to those stuffed inside, to the amusement of the crowd.

Some animal handlers were also skilled in pole vaulting and were daring enough to stand in the middle of the arena as they faced down a charging bear or lion only to pole vault over the enraged animal's head at the very last minute. Only after the confused beast swiped at thin air did it realize that the animal trainer had vaulted safely out of reach. Writer and historian Roland Auguet has also pointed out that there were plenty of brilliant non-violent acts in which circus animals were taught benign amusements, such as animal trainers being able to get up close and personal with docile big cats, even giving them a kiss or two, without the beast getting hostile in the process.

Elephants were also taught to "dance" and cavort about in an amusing manner. If legends and folktales are to be believed, there are also some amusing instances that occurred seemingly of their own accord. The tale of Androcles and the lion is one of them. This tale alleges that a lion befriended a condemned man in the arena rather than eating him. Although most today would say the story is a complete myth, in ancient Rome, it was related as if it might have actually occurred. In fact, Roman writer Apion (he was originally from Egypt but carried out his later work in Rome) insisted that he witnessed this event himself.

At any rate, according to legend, the condemned man Androcles had previously made nice to a lion when he was hiding out in the wilderness. Androcles was hiding in a cave when a lion popped up and displayed a wounded paw. Androcles took the bloody paw and pulled a giant thorn out of it. The lion was supposedly grateful and began to do Androcles's bidding, bringing meat back to the cave to sustain the man.

Androcles was captured shortly thereafter, however, and he was brought to the arena. The audience was supposedly shocked to see the lion who was ordered to attack the prisoner instead lick the prisoner's feet. A leopard was dispatched shortly thereafter, but the lion came bounding up and killed the leopard, fiercely protecting Androcles.

This is all well and good for myths and legends, but what do we know for sure about the animal-based games? For one thing, it's certain that a whole lot of animals were killed. It's documented in Roman records that on the opening day of the Roman Colosseum alone, some nine thousand animals were slaughtered. Even if this figure has been somehow inflated or exaggerated, it suggests that even if the real amount was less than nine thousand, it must have been at least in the thousands. And even if it were only one thousand slain animals, that number of dead beasts on the arena floor is hard to fathom.

Chapter 11 – Roman Theater in the Roman Games

"Likewise, we renounce your public shows just as we do their origins which we know were begotten of superstition, while we are completely aloof from those matters with which they are concerned. Our tongues, our eyes, our ears have nothing to do with the madness of the circus, the shamefulness of the theater, the brutality of the arena, the vanity of the gymnasium. How, then, do we offend you? If we prefer different pleasures, if we do not want to be amused, that is our loss—if loss there be—not yours."

-Christian writer, Tertullian

Romans loved theater. They had inherited the tradition from the Greeks and made it their own. But once they were made part of the Roman games, the length that the Romans would go to in their dramatic arts was startling. Oftentimes, the Romans would reenact famous plays in the arena with prisoners playing the part of condemned characters. Amy Zoll, in her book *Gladiatrix: The True Story of History's Unknown Woman Warrior*, rightfully described these reenactments as being the Roman equivalent of snuff films.

For even though the Romans did not have the technology to film these grotesque events, just like their modern counterpart, they were narratives in which a captive is forced to act out a part that ultimately leads to their demise. One favorite was reenactments of the myth of Orpheus, who supposedly could "soothe the savage beast." Promoters of the games would allow for reenactments that would put a condemned individual into the role of Orpheus, who was then forced to play the lyre in front of authentically savage beasts. Yet, when the condemned were made to play for lions, tigers, and bears in the arena, to the absolute delight of jeering spectators, rather than soothe the beasts' fury, they were rather predictably mauled to death. It must have been a pure streak of sadism that brought pleasure to see a man attempt to play a soothing musical instrument only to be struck down by a wild animal.

Having a condemned man play Hercules was rather popular too. At first glance, it might have seemed nice for a prisoner to be able to play a Greek hero like Hercules, but the end for Hercules was not very pretty. According to Greek myth, Hercules ended his own life by setting himself on fire. The grand finale of a portrayal of Hercules by the condemned would end in such a manner.

The prisoner would have been given a tunic covered in a highly flammable material called pitch and would then have been set ablaze for the final act. It was a jolly good show for the Roman spectators to watch as the burning man ran around the arena. These spectators were uncaring and completely oblivious to the pain and suffering the condemned must have felt in those last few moments of life.

Another fan favorite was to have a condemned woman play the part of Rome's version of the evil stepmother Dirce from the Greek play *Antiope*, who ends up perishing after being tied to the horns of a bull. This feat was reenacted live in the arena, with terrible results.

Another reenactment that shows the Romans' strange fascination with bulls is the mythological story of Pasiphae. Pasiphae is a character who is said to have had sex with a bull. It was this union that supposedly gave rise to the half-man/half-bull minotaurs of Greek mythology. In the Roman games, these scenes were disturbingly reenacted by having a condemned female prisoner stuffed inside a "wooden bull" while a real one was coerced into having its way with her. Needless to say, the victim of this bizarre stunt did not survive the bull's efforts. The Roman poet Martial made mention of this sorry event in his famous *Book of Spectacles.*

In reference to the event, Martial had declared, "Believe that Pasiphae was mated to the Cretan bull: we have seen it, the old-time myth is now believed! And let not Caesar, marvel at itself: the arena makes real for you whatever Fame sings of." Martial was basically saying that the Roman emperor (also known as a Caesar) was able to bring ancient myths and legends to life. Not only that, but he was also able to alter them since the mythic Pasiphae survived her mating with a bull to give birth to a minotaur. The unfortunate victim of this Roman orchestrated "game," however, most certainly did not survive.

Another grotesque rendition of this macabre theater was a theatrical presentation of the mythical Addis who, after being driven mad, famously castrated himself. It's unclear how a condemned prisoner might have been forced to castrate himself in front of thousands of screaming spectators in the arena, but the Romans were no doubt crafty enough to find a way. These shocking shows were typically held at midday—effectively the half-time of the Roman games—and were called *ludi meridian.*

As outrageous as these acts sound, many were clearly documented by Roman historians. One that was described in great detail was the execution of a condemned man by the name of Selurus, who was made to act out a part in one of these infamous Roman-styled snuff films.

According to Roman writer and historian Strabo, "And recently in my own time, a certain Selurus, called the 'son of Aetna' was sent up to Rome because he had put himself at the head of an army and for a long time had overrun the regions round about Aetna with frequent raids; I saw him torn to pieces by wild beasts at an appointed combat of gladiators in the Forum; for he was placed on a lofty scaffold, as though on Aetna, and the scaffold was made suddenly to break up and collapse, and he himself was carried down with it into cages of wild-beasts—fragile cages that had been prepared beneath the scaffold for that purpose."

This Selurus was apparently a thief who, after being condemned to death, had been made the star of an elaborate theatrical production. He was placed on a mock Mount Etna, complete with fake shrubbery and rock outcroppings. On top of this artificial mountain, Selurus was tied up and made to play the role of Prometheus. One familiar with mythology might recall that Prometheus was said to have given fire to man. For giving humanity that spark of knowledge, the gods punished Prometheus by chaining him up and allowing a bird to peck at his liver.

According to the legend, the bird would eat Prometheus's liver every single day, and every single night, it would grow back so that his agony would continue. As it pertains to this condemned thief, however, he wasn't assaulted by a bird but rather a bear that was suddenly released from a cage.

However, not everyone was so excited about these atrocities, as indicated by the famed Christian apologist Tertullian. In one of his epic "apologies," Tertullian railed against this form of entertainment.

He declared, "Of course, you are more devout in the seats of the amphitheater where, over human blood and the filth resulting from the tortures inflicted, your gods do their dancing and provide plots and stories for the guilty—except that the guilty, too, often assume the roles of your gods. We once saw Attis, that god from Pessinus, castrated, and a man who was being burned alive played the role of Hercules. Then, too, at the gladiators' midday performance, in the midst of the cruelties of the entertainment, we laughed at Mercury testing the dead with his red-hot iron. We watched Jupiter's brother too, hammer in hand, dragging away the corpses of the gladiators."

He then further stated, "When the face of one of your gods sits on a disreputable and infamous head [the head of a condemned prisoner], when an impure body of someone and up for the art in all effeminacy represents a Minerva or a Hercules, is not the majesty of your gods insulted and their deity dishonored? Yet you not merely look on, but applaud."

These remarks by this early Christian writer provide some rather fascinating insight into Roman culture. Tertullian was obviously not a fan of the Roman gods, yet even he was amazed that the Romans would be so depraved that they would seemingly mock their own gods by having condemned criminals play them in the arena. Not only that but Tertullian was also perplexed at the Roman practice of taking gods sacred to the Roman pantheon and having them murdered live before an audience.

Early Christians would indeed have recognized the irony of Romans committing deicide (homicide of a deity) since, from their viewpoint, it was the Romans who had crucified Christ. This, of course, is an awful lot to unpack from the reading of the remarks of one ancient Christian apologist, but it is indeed a rather stunning thing to contemplate.

For some reason, the Romans were more than happy to see heroes such as Hercules burnt to a crisp or Dirce gored by a bull. On occasion, they would even watch as the wings of the mythical Daedalus fail him so that he could be mauled by a bear. It is rather strange for a society to wish to take depictions of their most revered figures and have them ripped limb from limb.

Conclusion: The Roman Games Come to an End

The Roman Empire was the first of its kind, an empire that spanned continents and held far-flung regions together with both its might and its rule of law. In fact, the Romans were obsessed with the law. Before the Roman Empire was forged, there was the Roman Republic, which had fashioned a Senate full of lawmakers. In the centuries of the Roman Republic and even the Roman Empire as well, countless legislation was adopted in efforts to create rules and regulations for how society should be maintained.

For such a legalistic society, it is indeed rather shocking to learn of all the abuses that took place in the famed arenas. Many have pointed out how the games had their roots in funeral practices, in which gladiators fought for the honor of the recently deceased. Later detractors of the games would speculate that these actions stemmed from even older funerary rituals that involved nothing short of human sacrifice for the supposed restless spirits of the dead. It has been argued that the evolution of having men fight to the death was, therefore, just a smokescreen for the urge to spill human blood over the graves of the dearly departed.

At any rate, gladiator matches, along with chariot races, wild beast hunts, and all the rest, soon became standard fare in Rome. So much so that it was said that as long as the Roman public had "bread and circuses" on hand, they would be just fine. The games became more and more elaborate as time passed, both to keep the public entertained and to display Roman power to the masses. Even in the frontier cities of the empire, arenas were established so that frontier peoples could be shown Rome's military might.

In the end, however, the Roman games became increasingly depraved. It was common for Rome to throw criminals and others rejected by society to the lions, but the ways in which the condemned were killed became more devious as the years rolled by. So much so, in fact, that elaborate theatrical acts were created in which the condemned were given a starring role as great figures of Roman myths and legends only to be executed in the final scene.

Strangely, Rome became famous for not only public executions but also for having those they executed play the role of their greatest figures. Was Rome killing their undesirables, or were they killing their own greatness? Hercules, Jupiter, and Attis could all be desecrated and dispatched at any moment, sent to their deaths, and then hauled off by a mime dressed as deathly Charon.

It was only when Christianity became the dominant force in Rome that Roman intellectuals began to seriously question the Roman games. They began to wonder why the spilling of all this blood was necessary. And once such things were honestly considered, the games were no more.

Here's another book by Captivating History that you might like

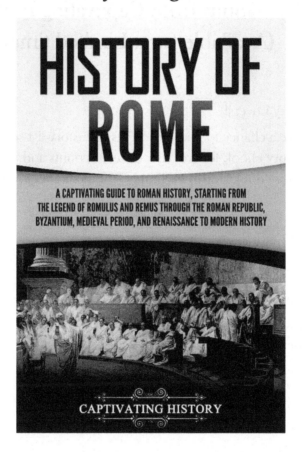

Free Bonus from Captivating History (Available for a Limited time)

Hi History Lovers!

Now you have a chance to join our exclusive history list so you can get your first history ebook for free as well as discounts and a potential to get more history books for free! Simply visit the link below to join.

Captivatinghistory.com/ebook

Also, make sure to follow us on Facebook, Twitter and Youtube by searching for Captivating History.

Appendix A: Further Reading and Reference

The Roman Games: A Sourcebook. Alison Futrell. 2006.

Arena: The Story of the Colosseum. John Pearson. 2013.

The Gladiator: The Secret History of Rome's Warrior. Alan Baker. 2002.

Gladiatrix: The True Story of History's Unknown Woman Warrior. Amy Zoll. 2002.

Cruelty and Civilization: The Roman Games. Roland Auguet. 1994.

Gladiators: Violence and Spectacle in Ancient Rome. Roger Dunkle. 2008.

Made in United States
North Haven, CT
01 March 2024

49429584R00059